The Confident Mother

The Confident Mother

a collection of learnings with excerpts of interviews from the 2015 The Confident Mother online conference

by

Sherry Bevan

from one mother to another,
Sherry

Practical Inspiration
PUBLISHING

First published in Great Britain by Practical Inspiration Publishing, 2015

© Sherry Bevan, 2015

The moral rights of the author have been asserted

ISBN (print): 978-1-910056-25-7
ISBN (ebook): 978-1-910056-26-4

Table of Contents

Foreword

The world of Parenting is one that we will never understand or feel adequately prepared for until that announcement by the person who delivers the baby that you have a boy or a girl. The voyage of discovery, into both you as a person as well as how to raise this tiny helpless being, is one of many highs and hopefully not too many lows. Everyone experiences parenthood differently, no two babies, no two mothers and no two families are ever the same, so how can we read up on what we should be doing, how we should be doing it, and what we should expect next? Parenting with confidence and trusting your inner instincts is something that isn't advertised enough in our society of quick-fix, fast answers, where the expectation is that we should all be able to do everything without asking for help.

Throughout this book, Sherry recounts the stories of the many fascinating interviews she has done with mothers from all walks of life who have all learned something from their own path through motherhood. Each one talks about their experiences in such a way that on every page there is an opportunity for the reader to feel connected with the person telling their story and to be able to apply their lessons within their own life. From scientific facts about human development, to heartfelt stories of love and tenderness in raising their own children, to inspiring stories of adjusting to life as a mother and finding a new career path that suits the whole family, or coping after divorce, this book is the first stepping stone to understanding how to become the mother you want to be; one that is good enough for your family.

While some books will promise quick-fix answers to the challenges of parenthood, and motherhood in particular, this book looks at building strong and lasting foundations in your own behaviour and actions, so that you can feel confident and well equipped to tackle the diversity of life as a mother. With key points at the end of every chapter and direct questions to ask yourself about your own personal situation, this book is sure to inspire you, support you and nurture you in being the confident mother you always hoped you would be. Sherry's approachable and down-to-earth nature shines through and enables the reader to feel empowered and ready for anything right from the very first chapter.

Dame Sarah Storey

Acknowledgements

This book would not have been possible without the wonderful community of mothers who have supported my journey to launch and run The Confident Mother conference, who joined me for the live interviews, who participated and continue to participate in the forum, and who opened their hearts and minds to hear the secrets being shared.

A special word of thanks to all the inspirational speakers who shared so many wonderful stories of their own journeys. Each and every one brought something unique and special to the microphone.

I'd particularly like to thank my family, my husband and my beautiful children who have been so patient in the last few weeks: 'Mummy, have you finished your book yet?'

My own personal journey to The Confident Mother has been supported along the way by some very special women:

Jean Rea, my NCT Breastfeeding Counsellor Tutor. It is through my studies with Jean that I learned so much more about myself.

My business coach, Fi Feehan. She is an amazing coach with a truly extraordinary ability to draw out what is lurking at the back of your mind, that you haven't quite found the confidence or the strength to articulate. I really am very grateful to Fi.

Alison Jones, my editor and book coach. I never could have done this without Alison's help and support. When it felt like an impossible task, she reminded me of the last two miles in the marathon, when your energy levels are flagging, you are in pain, you wonder if you can do it. Those last two miles are the hardest part – you have come so far, now you just need to finish. Just put one foot in front of another. She encouraged me to wear balls of steel. Thank you Alison.

A special thank you to all the mums – I never would have written this book if it wasn't for you.

Introduction

This book is for all mothers everywhere. It sets out my philosophy on life, and especially on being a mother. I am not the perfect mother and I do not aspire to be such. In the past, I described myself as a perfectionist, but now I know that it is impossible to be perfect; after all, whose 'perfect' would you be? Your 'perfect' will be different to your children's perfect which will be different to your mother's perfect. Perfection as a mother is impossible to attain. Today I am happy to be the **good enough** mother. If I am happy and my children are happy, that for me really is good enough. The realisation that happiness is more important than perfection has helped me become a Confident Mother.

The purpose of this book is to help you in your quest to be The Confident Mother. I came to motherhood late in life after a very successful, high-flying corporate career. I continued my successful career after my children and today I am running my own business, working very much to what I describe as my core purpose. So while I hope stay-at-home-mums will benefit greatly from reading this book, I want you to know from the start that my personal experience of being The Confident Mother is as a working mum. And in recent years, for me that's been a mum running her own business.

The book is based on an incredibly successful online conference that I first hosted in January 2015. I want this book to take you on a journey. In Section 1: **Introducing The Confident Mother** you will discover my own personal journey and how I came to be The Confidence Guide, working as a coach and mentor to help other women in their careers and businesses. You will understand how and why I decided to create the online conference, and the value it created for so many women.

In Section 2: **Interviews** I will share highlights from the conference, using excerpts from more than 20 interviews with inspirational mothers and mothering experts, conducted over the three weeks. Each interviewee brought something special and unique to the conference.

At the end of each interview, I have summarised the key learnings, and where appropriate I have noted additional resources which you might find useful.

I have tried to structure the interviews in chronological order, starting with the very early days of being a mother, through to older children and teenagers. Next come the more specific motherhood experiences, e.g. the adoptive mother, the single mother; I explore your options if you are a mum ready to go back to work or set up a business; and finally we discover tips and strategies to help us have more confidence in the way we feel and project ourselves, through our health, our dress and our presence.

Finally, in Section 3: **Additional Resources,** you have an opportunity to continue your own personal journey. Maybe you are already The Confident Mother. (In which case I would love to hear from you for the next event, contact me at srb@sherrybevan.co.uk).

Over the years I have invested £000s into my own personal development. And no matter how many courses I attend, TED lectures that I watch, books that I read or podcasts that I hear, there is always some new nugget of wisdom or knowledge to explore. Therefore it is my belief that regardless of how far along the path you have travelled to The Confident Mother, you will find the exercises and activities useful, whether or not they are ones that you have tried before. Throughout the book, I have highlighted additional resources on my website. For example, if you know that you are an auditory learner, many of the activities and exercises are available as audio downloads.

Many of the additional resources are available at the website, www.theconfidentmother.co.uk, however I also include books by the authors who have most influenced me on my journey.

I am a bookworm; over many years of studying how to be a good enough mother, I have acquired a huge pile of books. If there is a book that has really made an impact on you or influenced the way that you behave as a mother or with your children, I would LOVE to hear from you.

If you are a Dad taking a quick browse and wondering if this is the book for a mother that you know, do check out the **Bibliography** in **Additional Resources**. I am pretty confident that something on the list will be just the book you are looking for (as well as this one of course!).

I am always happy to have your feedback and comments: come and find me hanging out in **The Confident Mother** group on Facebook.

Sherry Bevan
September 2015

Introducing The Confident Mother

My Journey

My journey to The Confident Mother is one of big ups and big downs, like so many of us. I had children late in life – I was an older mum. You are classed as an older mum when you hit 35. Considering the average age in the UK to start a family today is 32, 35 is not so very old. However biologically we are 'meant' to have babies much younger. The use of contraception and the freedom to be a working woman have influenced our breeding patterns. For years, I didn't want to have children. I didn't see the point. It's not that I didn't like children – when we visited friends' houses, their kids ended up climbing all over me. I never understood why but a couple of friends told me it was because I listened properly to them, and I talked to them in a 'grown-up' way.

So the big ups and downs before that…

My childhood years

When I was about 12 or 13, my parents divorced. I was devastated. Life was turned upside down. I was a real

Daddy's girl and I didn't know how to cope. I was of an age to understand everything that was going on; it's not nice watching your parents become bitter and antagonistic towards each other.

My father worked hard – he worked for IBM in the 1970s. When I was young, I thought he was wonderful and knew everything. I remember the day that I was shocked to learn that he didn't know everything – we were in a paper shop and there was a Chinese newspaper. The headline photo caught my eye and I asked him what the headline meant – he didn't know! His work ethic left its mark on me – he is a bright and intelligent man and expected me to be the same. At school I worked hard and aimed high.

When my parents first split up, my mum left home and lived with her new boyfriend. A few months later Dad moved out, and Mum moved back into the house with her boyfriend. We did not get on. Not at all. Not one little bit.

The troubled teenage years

Throughout my teenage years, I was good academically and I always had high expectations for myself. I chose not to go to university; in hindsight I am not really sure why. It is clear to me now that I was a troubled teenager struggling with depression and lacking in confidence. At the time I justified my decision because I didn't want to leave my mum all alone after the divorce. I went on to further education closer to home so that I could be with my mother and family. It was around this time that my beloved aunt was in a serious road accident. She was in intensive care for several months. Visiting intensive care was a horrible experience for a teenager who was struggling with life anyway.

Not long afterwards, another family tragedy struck: my Mum's boyfriend died unexpectedly at work with a heart attack. To be honest I don't remember much about this time, but I do remember the police knocking at the front door.

It was a tough time as a teenager. I grew up fast. I think this is reflected today in my strong independence and anti-conformist attitude to life. Life has thrown everything it can at me. In the words of Chumbawamba:

I get knocked down
But I get up again
You're never going to keep me down

With so much stuff going on in the family, I didn't apply to UCAS clearing for a place at university. Bizarrely, when I reflect back, nobody from my 6th-form college encouraged me to apply; but maybe they'd given up on me. I was taking a lot of time off sick – stress and depression, I now realise.

As a teenager I'd planned that I would meet my ideal husband at the age of 23, maybe get married at 27, and then after that… well, I hadn't thought beyond that. I didn't start dating boys until I was 16 or 17, when I was at 6th-form college.

I met the love of my life there. Teenage sweethearts, and still going strong 28 years later. We shared the same taste in music… once we started going out together, that was it.

We had been going out together for a year when we had a serious road traffic accident. My leg was crushed between a car and the scooter that I was riding pillion. I was in full leg plaster for five months and on crutches for six months. I was badly scarred in that accident – the cut on my left thigh was two inches wide and an inch deep, damaging the muscle itself. Life knocked me down but I got up again. (A few months after that I was back on the scooter, and in time I took my motorbike test and bought a fast typical 'boy racer' motorbike, the ZX-6R.)

Work Hard Play Hard

I married my teenage sweetheart a few years later when I was 23. We bought our first flat together; after a year (this is in the late 80s), the value of our flat had skyrocketed and we relocated to a London suburb which suited me better for work. I was an ambitious career girl. This was a fantastic period in my life: I felt grown-up, clever, sophisticated and my career progressed fast. I worked long hours, learning fast, for a company that invested in its staff. I worked hard and I partied hard. Not at all conducive to being a mother, but quite honestly at that time, being a mum was the furthest thing from my mind.

I was lucky to be in at the start of 'technology' when technology in the workplace was moving incredibly quickly. It was a fantastic opportunity for me – there I was, a smart intelligent woman who understood the technology yet had great communication and interpersonal skills. I was the epitome of the new era of technologists. No longer were IT people the oddballs who rarely emerged from their tiny backroom offices. We were coming out into the open and communicating with our users.

Around 1993 I found a passion for cycling, which was great because it meant that I had something else to focus on outside work. However in 1994, another tragedy. I had a serious racing accident. I came off my bike and landed head first. I suffered an almost fatal head injury which affected my ability to cope for about two years. I found it difficult to concentrate, to remember simple words such as 'spoon' or 'fork'. I always watch the Tour de France and that same year there was a horrific finish line pile-up involving several riders. A young French sprinter called Laurent Jalabert was front-page news; photographed with blood streaming down his face. Just like I had been a few days earlier. I started to follow his progress as he recovered. The next year, 1995, was his best year ever, proving that there is strength through adversity. He inspired me to get back on the bike and get on with life. I have been his No. 1 fan ever since.

I nearly burnt out after 11 years at Arthur Andersen. By 1997, I realised I was at breaking point, working 8am to 8pm on a regular basis. I quit before I had a job to go to. On the surface, I may have looked self-assured and confident. But underneath, I was a swirling morass of suicidal and self-harming thoughts. As I write these words, bam! It's powerful, it's emotional. This is the first time I have acknowledged those thoughts out loud. Those teenager years were still haunting me.

My next job was in a bank. I hated it. I was working 9am to 5pm, and not having enough work to fill those hours. I thought I was going to die from boredom. I moved on – to an international law firm; a role that I came to love. I was at the law firm for 10 years. Again, several promotions came my way. This was a great role for me – the business application of technology and the communication between technology and the business. Right up my street as a natural born communicator.

Cycling was still a big part of my life. A couple of months earlier, I had started to work with a cycling coach – I wanted to be at optimum performance levels to compete at the Three Peaks Cyclo-Cross event. Very quickly I started to see amazing positive benefits to my performance; no longer was I struggling at the back of the cycling group on club runs. I was at the front, feeling very comfortable, with people calling out for me to 'slow down'. What, me? I'm going too fast? Yet it felt so relaxed. I was starting to feel fantastic. Then the foot and mouth epidemic hit the UK. The Three Peaks Race was cancelled.

The decision to have children

Then in February 2001, aged 38, my life changed, practically overnight. My Nan died. I had been very close to my Nan. She lived in Cornwall but she'd always told me (perhaps a bit naughty of her), that I'd been her favourite grand-daughter. My Nan had been a great influence on my life. She was an eccentric artist – very different to your typical grand-mother. She wore high heels and trendy clothes – I was very close to her and we wrote long letters to each other. I always wanted her to be proud of me. Standing at the graveside at the funeral service, a fleeting thought struck me... 'now she'll never see my children.'

It was IN that moment that I thought to myself, 'I want children.'

I had read that it takes on average six months to get pregnant; my thought process was 'we could start trying now [in May], I'd get through the cyclo-cross race season [which started in September] and aim for Top 3 in the London League, get pregnant, and be back on my bike in time for the following year's cyclo-cross season and enter the Three Peaks next year instead.' Brilliant planning. Except that Mother Nature didn't read the plan.

I started the summer race season. I did a mountain bike race in June and my coach and I planned my race strategy very carefully: ride moderately for the first half, push hard in the second. It was a hot sunny day. The gun went and we were off – 'Oh my word, this is hard work today.' I couldn't even keep up with the bunch. I wondered whether it was my asthma or hayfever affecting me. I was struggling and yet I should have been flying, based on my performance on the road in the previous 3 or 4 weeks. I had eaten well, hydrated well… I just couldn't understand why I was finding it so hard. A few days later I realised I was pregnant.

I was shocked that I had fallen pregnant SO quickly. It must have been the first time we'd had sex without contraception. When I told our GP he replied, 'Well that's the average and it takes into account very fit people and very unfit people. You've fallen pregnant straight away – look how healthy and fit you are.' I was somewhat peeved but hey ho, I'm pregnant, and then the morning sickness began. Moving swiftly on to the time after birth…

The pain of postnatal depression

My labour was a typical cascade of interventions. I was 12 days overdue when I went to hospital to be induced. One thing led to another and I had a baby girl by emergency c-section.

Once the decision was made, I couldn't stop crying. I was exhausted both mentally and physically. I felt I'd failed. When Laura arrived, I barely managed a smile.

Postnatal depression (PND) started almost immediately. The physical recovery took a long time. After the birth, everything hurt – I was swollen, sore and bruised inside. Sitting down for too long hurt and much of those early days was spent sitting down to breastfeed.

At first I didn't realise I had depression. I had some bad days, some good. There were some weeks when every day was a bad day.

I felt exhausted – I expected to be tired feeding a baby through the night, but I was so tired it hurt. My whole body was racked with pain. Yet I couldn't sleep.

There were days when I couldn't stop crying for no reason. I felt as though I couldn't cope. I didn't want to eat, wash, get dressed… it wasn't that I didn't want to, I just couldn't be bothered and didn't see the point. I didn't ever contemplate suicide in that I didn't come up with a plan (I didn't have the energy), but I did want life to stop and for me to climb into a dark box somewhere.

My concentration was shot to pieces. I felt angry, guilty and responsible for everything. I couldn't make decisions – even simple ones like tomato sauce or meat sauce with the pasta. My sex drive was zero. At times I thought I was going mad… my behaviour was that of a mad woman.

I joined my local mother and baby group, which helped. Exercise helped. When I was feeling bad, my husband would force me out on my bike or to the gym.

I knew that I had PND for a long time before I plucked up the courage to admit it. I had this really strong urge to talk through my experiences and feelings but I didn't have anybody that I felt I could talk to; my husband didn't want to know. He didn't want to deal with it – we were both in a bad place.

The first time I visited my doctor was 8 months later. My GP was fantastic – talking to him, acknowledging that I was ill and needed help, was enough to make me feel much better. Even so, a few weeks later, I was back, and he prescribed anti-depressants. I took anti-depressants for about 5 months. In retrospect I should have continued for longer, because I continued to have bad days for several months. In all, it was almost two years after Laura's birth before I felt fully recovered.

I had my second daughter a year later and I did have PND again. By then I'd built a good network of friends and supporters through NCT who knew I'd been ill before. Having their support helped get me through it the second time.

Starting my journey to The Confident Mother

Once I started to train as a breastfeeding counsellor, I researched postnatal depression, and I realised that I had suffered from antenatal depression in my first pregnancy: the intense mood swings and even before that the thoughts and desire to self-harm were undoubtedly signs. Yet, despite these two episodes of postnatal depression, I was promoted both times while I was on maternity leave.

I first developed an interest in training as a breastfeeding counsellor after my first daughter was born. A natural researcher and nature girl, I recognised that many mums were giving up breastfeeding before they wanted to, because they received poor support or misinformation. The PND meant that I was not well enough to contemplate studying until two years after I first spoke to my tutor. However those initial contacts prompted me to join the NCT and to start volunteering. After volunteering in small ways, handing out goody bags to parents at the local festival, I took on various roles including newsletter editor, press and publicity officer, website manager, branch chair, etc. Later I volunteered at a senior level as the London Regional Coordinator. Even now, I continue to run workshops for other volunteers and NCT practitioners.

After both my maternity leaves, I returned to work. I was sad to leave my children but I was also delighted to go back to work – being a mum at home was such hard work. Being able to go to the toilet in peace! Drinking a cup of tea while it was still hot! The small delights.

For a while my husband worked too, however we realised that he was working simply to pay the childminder. Simple mathematics, I was earning 3x his salary; we realised it didn't make parenting or financial sense, and he gave up work to become a stay-at-home dad. Like many mums, he went back to work once the girls started at primary school.

Following on from the interview with Toni Brodelle, I reflected long and hard on the two questions she posed that help us to understand how our emotional blueprint has been shaped:

- When you were younger, whose love did you crave the most? Answer instinctively, don't think about it.

- In order to have to experience that love, what did I have to do and who did I have to be? Love could be respect, praise, appreciation, time… love comes in many forms.

I thought that working hard, being clever and being successful was what I needed to do to be loved. For me, the effortless effort of running a business I love and that I'm passionate about didn't fit comfortably for a long time. How can I be a 'good person' when work is not hard? How can it be valuable? I have always been successful and confident, yet at the same time I have not taken risks that maybe I would have done were it not for the fact that I don't like to fail. My success has been because I am smart and clever and learn fast and I have chosen wisely, but it's also because I have not allowed myself to fail. If I thought I might fail, I wouldn't take the risk.

Life has changed.

I now work as a confidence coach and specialise in helping mums to make life-changing decisions such as going back to work after a career break or setting up their own business. Although my body and my mental health have taken some battering over the years, my emotional wellbeing is strong. My life events have given me an inner strength and confidence that allow me to nurture and inspire other women.

How can you be the Confident Mother?

It's not magic. I can't turn you into The Confident Mother. You need to have the wish, the vision, the desire that in turn creates the actions to allow you to achieve your goal.

What I *will* provide you with is a collection of inspirational stories and learnings. Take your first steps today to being The Confident Mother.

What we learn from the she-wolf

I have always been a nature girl. I love being outside, I love being in the woods, I love animals, I love fresh air, when I'm running I prefer trails to pavements, when I used to race on my bike, I preferred muddy cyclo-cross to tarmac.

However for many years I was also the epitome of the Career Girl. High level job in a professional services firm, swiftly being promoted through the ranks. I worked hard and I played hard. I enjoyed wearing a smart suit to work. I enjoyed being respected for my knowledge and expertise. But to me, being relaxed and comfortable meant wearing jeans, a sweatshirt and my boots.

So when I first became a mother, it was nature that I turned to for inspiration. I love wolves. Yes, truly, I do. I wanted to be a mum the way that a female wolf is a mum. The wolf pack has one dominant male and one dominant female. The alpha female is the one 'allowed' to bear pups and she truly looks after them and nurtures them. She doesn't need books to know what to do. She trusts in her instincts.

The mummy wolf was the inspiration to me to be the mother that I am. A mother that is gentle with her babies (or pups) yet fiercely protective. A mother for whom feeding is enjoyable and essential. Sleeping together makes perfect sense to keep my babies safe and warm.

But more than anything, as a mother, when I'm troubled or unsure or feeling distressed, or don't know what I am supposed to do, I don't turn to a parenting book. No, I turn to my mummy wolf. What would she do? What would her mothering instincts tell her to do? What are my instincts telling me to do?

The problem with our society, the society that we live in today, is that too many of us can no longer hear our instincts telling us what to do. We do all know instinctively how to be The Confident Mother. We all know that when your baby cries, you pick her up and cuddle her or put her to the breast, or rock her, or shhh, shhh, shhh to her. We all know that instinctively. Honestly we do… it's just that in our society our instincts have been smothered, covered in a thick fog, a blanket of 'don't spoil your baby', 'don't make a rod for your own back', 'children should be seen not heard' or 'babies need to cry to exercise their lungs'. Seriously? Do you think there is any other creature in the world that 'needs to exercise its lungs' in order to survive?

It's all those 'shoulds'. All those rules. All that misinformation. Misknowledge. Misexpertise. Have you seen how many parenting books you can buy on Amazon? 89,210 when I last looked! Those books aren't just written to make your life easy and to help you to tackle your parenting challenges; those books are written to promote a particular author's philosophy. (And yes, I'm here to promote my philosophy too.)

If we just listened to our instincts, and did what we felt was right, wouldn't that be more powerful? More effective? More natural? Back in the days of living in caves, don't you think the cavewoman just KNEW how to look after her baby?

Different mammal species have evolved different survival strategies. Altricial species such as rabbits, mice, and cats give birth to many offspring in a litter. The litters are hidden in a safe nest or den. Their babies are helpless at birth, often blind and hairless, and unable to cling to their mother. They do not need to feed often as their mothers provide high-fat milk which takes a long time to digest. Precocial species such as deer, cows, and horses give birth to just one or two babies which are well developed at birth. They can usually see well, they are able to walk shortly after being born and therefore they are physically able to stay close to their mother. This means that they can feed frequently; their milk is relatively low in fat but high in calories, designed to suit this lifestyle. Then we have the primate species such as gorillas and orang-utans. Their young are well-developed at birth, can cling on to and travel with their mother, and feed frequently on low-fat, high-calorie milk.

What about humans? Where does our survival strategy fit? In some ways we fit with the precocial pattern because we give birth typically to one or two young at a time. Our babies have some well-developed senses at birth (hearing and touch). Our milk is high in calories and low in fat and therefore our babies need to feed frequently. What is different though is that our babies do not have the ability to cling on and they cannot walk to stay close to us. They are totally dependent on someone to keep them close, provide warmth and protection and give them frequent access to milk. Human babies could not survive without the constant presence of a care giver. They are designed to be close to their mum, both day and night. Dame Sarah Storey's interview emphasises this aspect of being a mum. In the last 20 years, neuroscience knowledge has increased significantly. Today we know that for optimal brain development we need to hold our babies close. Attachment in the early days, months and years is essential for our emotional well-being and resilience as adults. Babies need consistency and repetition. And when we listen to our instincts, this is what mothers naturally do.

And that is partly the reason I have written this book – to bring us back to our instincts, to natural parenting, but also so that you know that you don't need to be the perfect parent all of the time. That a baby's needs are pretty simple – it's not complicated and if you can reflect on mummy wolf, and what she would do in a similar situation, you can be sure you'll be doing a good enough job.

This is something I often refer to in my breastfeeding classes: if you don't know what to do, if you don't know whether it's ok to pick up your baby, to cuddle her, to put her to the breast again, think about that mummy wolf (in fact I tend to use mummy cat and her kittens because I recognise that for a lot of people, a mummy wolf is not that appealing).

Can you be a feminist and a mother?

Before I had children, I associated being a feminist with being a strong woman who stood up not just for her rights but for others too. Who wasn't afraid to say what she thought. Who was not going to be put down by bullies or society.

Somehow, in the depths of my mind, I did not associate being a feminist with being a mother. In fact I'll go one further, I assumed you couldn't be a mother if you were a feminist. Yet I was not conscious of these thoughts. When I started on my journey to The Confident Mother, I kept being pulled by this conflict. What's going on? I am a strong feminist and I am a good mother. Why can't I allow the two people to appear in the same room? I am strident at times (my husband will attest to that) – I am vocal – I am passionate – I get angry at injustice and inequality and I allow my anger to show. In my emotions, in my expressions, in my feelings, and most importantly in my actions. By that, I don't mean I throw bricks at the TV when some grey-suited male tells me all about why it's so important to protect the family unit, and why we need to invest more funding in breastfeeding support (all the while, NHS England has withdrawn its funding to support my local breastfeeding drop-in). No, I mean I stand up and do something positive.

Before I wrote this chapter, I talked to my coach, Fi. I wanted to explore this disassociation and therefore conflict in my head about feminism and motherhood. It so happens that Fi studied sociology and she pointed out that nowhere in her readings and studies, even among the most lesbian writings, does it say anywhere at all that you can't be both a mother and a feminist.

Where has this assumption come from? It's not even a conscious thought. But it is lurking there because it's ambushed me from time to time.

I recall my own mother – I guess probably a typical working mother in the 60s/70s, doing some part-time jobs here and there, below her intellectual 'status'. My mum left school after GCEs. She had various jobs – she didn't really have a career as such for many years. Later, in my late teenage years, she trained as a driving school instructor, and very good she was too. I don't really think of her as a feminist.

Then I think of my maternal grandmother. My mum was the youngest of five daughters, though one of her sisters died very young. My mum's dad (my maternal grandfather) died when my mum was very young and so she never really knew her dad. Gran brought up her children all by herself – tough times because the welfare state was not what it is now. I remember Mum telling me tales of Gran working in a biscuit factory, not exactly well-paid work.

On my father's side, my grandmother was one of life's eccentrics. An artist who would happily live in a garret, she had worked in the hotel trade for much of her working life. She married my grandfather when she was quite young but the marriage didn't work out. She left the family and left her children with their dad. Even today that would be a shocking story, and it was even more so in the 1950s. Nan remarried a few years later; her new husband was 20 years her junior. Another shocking story even by the standards of today's newspapers.

In many ways, my Nan was the feminist who did what was right for her. But she 'abandoned' her family… I wonder if it is simply the language here that is confusing me so much? Is my vision of the 'perfect' mother wrapped up in a romantic idea of a warm, round woman, who doesn't have a strident, aggressive bone in her body? Is my messed-up definition of a feminist tripping over my vision of the perfect mother?

Why The Confident Mother?

I created a successful business performance consultancy in 2012 and specialised in working with law firm technology teams. I had been working in this niche sector for many years. I was well known, both in the UK and US, in the legal IT community. I had worked both in-house and for an out-sourcing provider before I set up my own business. It made sense to work in this niche.

One of the main reasons that prompted me to finally set up my own business was that I wanted more quality time with my children. I wanted more flexible working hours, particularly as my girls were getting closer to secondary school education. Until this point, my husband had been the stay-at-home parent. However I wanted to be more involved in their schooling; to be more available to help with homework and get involved in the school.

After about two years, although I enjoyed my business, there was something missing. Something not quite right. I loved talking to new or potential clients and exploring ways in which we could work together. It's such a buzz when a new client signs on the dotted line. But it wasn't enough. I wasn't passionate about it. I joined a mastermind group to get help and support, and rekindle the love for my business.

Slowly it dawned on me: all my years of supporting mothers in the workplace, supporting mothers as an NCT volunteer, supporting mothers as a breastfeeding counsellor, and supporting mothers through my coaching work… THIS is where I need to focus ALL my time and attention.

I want women to feel powerful. I believe you gain power through confidence; through knowledge; through self-understanding. Being powerful is about being in control of your life. I specialise in helping women who are at a crossroads in their life and want support to make life-changing decisions: promotion to the board; relocation to another country; going back to work after a career break; setting up a new business; growing the business to new levels of growth and success.

I have always felt very strongly that working mums get a raw deal. Often, being away from the workplace means mums lose confidence. Even before becoming a mum, many women lack confidence compared to their male peers and do not put themselves forward for promotion; or they apply for roles which do not stretch and challenge them.

I wanted to create The Confident Mother conference to share inspirational stories and practical tips from the frontline, actionable stories and ideas, so that mums everywhere, and especially working mums, take confidence that good enough really is good enough; you don't need to be the perfect mother. I wanted mums to feel inspired, motivated, lifted... I want mums to raise their self-esteem and boost their confidence so that they can take control of their lives.

Did I succeed? Let the participants tell their story.

The Confident Mother online conference is now an annual fixture to brighten up the start of your year in January. Get in touch if you have been inspired by a mother in any sphere of life and think she will bring something special to other mums.

—

Section Two
Interviews

Epitome of The Confident Mother

Dame Sarah Storey

She says 'Juice bar, juice bar' and taps me on the chest.

I was very excited to talk to Dame Sarah Storey. I'm a big cycling fan and she is one of my heroes. She is one of GB's best ever Paralympic athletes and she is also one of Britain's top female cyclists. Sarah continues to race at the top level – the only time we could fit this interview into her busy racing and travel schedule was one Sunday lunchtime, and I really appreciated her taking time away from her family. This interview is one of my highlights from the whole series because everything that Sarah does and stands for fits so closely with my ethos and philosophy about being a good enough mother. I also greatly admired her stance and the pioneering role that she is taking for mothers in sport. It was an absolute delight talking to Sarah.

Sarah started with a brief overview of her sporting career.

SS: As an international athlete, this is my 24th year on the British team. I started out as a 14-year-old swimmer and went to my first Games in Barcelona in 1992. In 2005 I switched sports and I've been on the British cycling team for almost the last ten years.

London 2012 was my most successful event. I won four gold medals: two on the track at the velodrome and two on the road at Brands Hatch.

SB: *Such an amazing long career at the top level – how do you sustain that power and that ambition for so long?*

SS: As a kid, I remember watching a young swimmer called Sarah Hardcastle at the 1984 Los Angeles Games. She was 15 at the time. Sarah won a silver and a bronze medal. Ever since, I wanted to be an international athlete and compete for Great Britain. I wanted to emulate Sarah but go one better and win gold. Sarah sparked that idea of being a precocious talent. I've been fit and well enough to do so, though it's not without its ups and downs. I've always had that drive and I love what I do. I'm institutionalised to sport, I suppose. Being able to represent your country, the opportunity to win gold medals; that chance that you might be on top of the rostrum again; watching the flag raise as the national anthem is played: it gives me shivers thinking about the possibility which definitely keeps the motivation.

SS: *When we watch a British athlete stand up on that podium and the flag goes up, we get shivers too. I can't imagine how it feels knowing that you're the one that's done that.*

SS: It's incredible. It's the first point that you get to be quiet and think your own thoughts. After you've finished the race, it goes crazy for a while but when you're stood on the rostrum, you start to think about the troubles you've been through, the people that have helped you, the way that you've prepared; the event goes through your mind. It's a really short time that you're stood there listening to the anthem but all these things come flooding back. And you remember how everyone has a piece of that medal because you can't do it by yourself.

We moved on to talking about Sarah's experiences as a mum ...

SB: *As an NCT breastfeeding counsellor, I was delighted to read in a recent interview in* The Guardian *that you're still breastfeeding your daughter who is 19 months now.*

SS: Yes, it's an incredible journey. I had always intended to breastfeed but the length of time was open to negotiation. It's created some challenges but none impossible to overcome. When I first started training, Louisa would be at the velodrome in the stands with my husband. If she wouldn't take the bottle of expressed milk, she really wanted me. So I would nip upstairs in between efforts to give her a quick feed when she was three, four, five months old.

We went down the baby-led weaning route and for the first couple of months, milk was still the main source of nourishment. As she started to eat more, she's continued to breastfeed as well. It helps her in the night when she sleeps with me. We travel so much and stay in strange places. We can be changing hotels on a daily basis for up to week. She has that consistency of always having me; it creates challenges but it's not logistically impossible.

She sleeps really well wherever we are. It helps with her jet lag. I think breastfeeding plays a huge part in that process and it's consistency for her. We say she's 'plugged in and rebooting'. She's getting into that toddler phase – all the big emotions getting too much for her, yet she can calm down very quickly. She says, 'Juice bar, juice bar!' and taps me on the chest. She'll cover me up and make snoring noises because 'juice bar' is sleeping.

SB: *Sleeping together and breastfeeding, you are giving her that consistency of always having you, which is so important as a mother.*

SS: Definitely. I read a lot of gentle parenting books when I was pregnant. The correlation between confident children and independent children. She's dependent on me but she's also very independent. When she feels emotional and needs extra support, I'm that person. She's also very attached to her dad and she can fall asleep just as easily for him. She's devoted to her main care givers: to my husband, to me, and to my parents.

Those 19 months have flown by. We all get more sleep because of the route that we've chosen. We chose it because we knew we'd be flying around the world once I got back racing. We wanted to make sure it wasn't scary for Louisa; we wanted to make sure it was something she could enjoy. She loves planes, she loves going around the world, she loves the adventure. She has that consistency, of being where she wants to be at night, with me, or during the day when she needs a quick feed.

SB: *In the Dorothy Marlen and Miriam McCaleb interviews, they talk about the importance of having that bond with your child and how your child's brain develops in those first two or three years; how 'attachment parenting', if you use a label, can help.*

SS: I read a lot about how the child's brain develops. Our infants are so immature when they're born compared to other mammals and it's our job to nurture them throughout their first years.

SB: *What milestones has Louisa reached?*

SS: She was stood up on her feet when she was eight months old, pulling herself around. She never let go until she was 14 months but once she let go, she just ran and now she doesn't stop running. She's very confident in the water without flotation aids. She loves swimming. We've been swimming every week since she was six weeks old. She goes in the water every day on training camps abroad because we're in warmer climates.

She's talking, she has new words every day. We spend a lot of time in Spain and she's learnt her first Spanish words, *gracias, buenas noches* and *hola*.

SS: In France, I'll be talking to her in French; we have a French rider on our team so we'll be exposing her to those cultural and language differences as often as we can. It's an education. A young brain is such a sponge.

SB: *You manage the tricky balance of being a mum AND a full time athlete by taking her with you to all your races and training camps.*

SS: Because of the breastfeeding it has to be that way, so we haven't spent a night apart. We won't spend a night apart until she's ready. She has a cot which has been adjusted so it's a co-sleeping cot. We bought a super king-size bed for when she is bigger, so there's plenty of space for the three of us. When she's ready, she'll be able to sleep apart from me. We'll go with her lead.

Taking her everywhere with us has been better for me as well. It's not just about Louisa, it's about me knowing that she's well looked after. Not that I don't trust anybody else, but as mum, you think you're her first point of call. If she really hurts herself, 'Mummy, Mummy', is what she says. It gives me confidence and reassurance when she's right there next to me and I can sleep deeply too.

SB: *What has been the best thing about becoming a mum?*

SS: It's been fun. Now we see the world through the eyes of a toddler which is hilarious. It seems routine to us but bicycles are really exciting. You can shout 'Go, go, go!' at them. The wheels do things, and Allen keys and spanners… she's always picking up the tools and fixing the bike. She has this whole new world to explore every day and it's been so much fun to see that happen.

Before you have children, you don't understand the enormity and the miracle. Even if you've fallen pregnant easily, it's a miracle because that little person is born and you look after them for everything. It's absolutely amazing, it's an absolutely incredible thing. I'm so chuffed and I couldn't recommend it more.

SB: *What have been the challenges for you as a mum?*

SS: There are times when teeth are coming through and she's screaming. Louisa was up every hour on Christmas Eve because she had five teeth appearing at the same time but that's far more difficult for her than it is for me. I've never minded. I guess it's the frustrations when you know how you can make things better but her mouth is too sore. It passes quickly.

The challenges are around other people's approach – it's not always the easiest thing combining motherhood and sport. There are discussions that have to happen around taking a child with you to World Championships, having to stay separately to the British team because you can't stay in the team hotel with your family. Those things are difficult and you have to find ways round them – to do your job, ultimately, which is winning medals while not neglecting your child.

Sometimes those discussions need to happen more and sooner. That understanding that as a mother you're not being awkward by saying, 'I really have to be with my child.' It's a life necessity. At a year and a half, she is still a baby really. What you give to them in their early years will help shape their entire life. If for the first four or five years of their life you can't be without them, and they have to stay with you every night, that shouldn't be questioned. It should be absolutely accepted because that child is as important as winning a medal, more important in fact.

Those discussions are the most difficult ones... the additional requirements and logistical arrangements needed to keep both sides of your life happy.

SB: *There probably aren't many mothers on the British teams for that to be more widely accepted?*

SS: Absolutely true, Shelly Rudman's just had her second baby, she's on the British skeleton bob team. She has a husband who competes too. Barney doesn't compete now so it's a different situation; he's around all the time for Louisa.

There are plenty of good models of how it can work very well, for example the American soccer team. They have nannies travelling with the team so that the mothers can be with their children. The nannies look after the children during squad training sessions and competitions. There are guidelines on how to manage that, to ensure that the squad is respected and that the children are respected as well. They're given access to their mothers all the time, with the understanding that for a certain number of hours in the day, the nannies take over.

It's a team of women so it's completely different to the mixed teams of other sports. The footballers can concentrate on doing their job and they know their children are well looked after. They go back to them in the evenings as any working parent would. How that works in a mixed team is something that we could expand upon and improve.

SB: *Do you think the Americans are more accepting of that necessity to be with your child in their early years?*

SS: I don't know whether culturally they're any further forward than we are. They have the means in football to do so. They've had more mothers competing for the US over the years.

SB: *They've had to adapt.*

SS: Absolutely, and the finances are different. If you're in a sport where you can earn good money as an athlete, you're going to end up with more female athletes who are older. Therefore more female athletes who are mothers. National Lottery funding appeared in the UK which allowed athletes to be full time from 1996. Less than 20 years later we have women in their 30s, who are thinking about starting a family.

They've been able to have a longer career because they've been able to train full-time. They've had that back-up and medical support for illness or injuries, a more structured approach.

We're going to see more athletes who start families. Not all athletes come back stronger. Physiologically it's possible to come back stronger and I certainly benefited but some are incredibly sick all through pregnancy and can't train. They don't get the physiological benefits afterwards because their body is wrecked from nine months of sickness. Everybody is different and everybody's return to fitness is different. Some never make it. But most women [athletes] in the UK appear to retire in order to have children.

SB: *Perhaps you are a trend setter here and you're setting the model for what might be coming in future years for British athletes.*

SS: I think that's the case. Most of us work with male dominated coaches and managerial structure for our sport. I have no problem working with any gender coach or manager provided they do a good job. It's about those open conversations: 'I'm not being awkward here but my child still needs me.' Every child develops at a different rate and every child will become independent at a different time. There's no right or wrong way to get your child to sleep through the night or to be more independent or to cope without you for a number of days. It's easier for male athletes to leave their children with their mothers at home; mum is the most important

part of that family unit when it comes to children set-
tling, being happy and sleeping.

Once we accept that it's a different role for a father
compared to a mother within sport, we can move
forwards with how we manage that. At the moment
there's a bit of, 'Well the men can go off for three
weeks and leave their children, they can cope emotionally, therefore the mothers should cope.' It's not
about the mother coping; it's about how that child
copes with mum gone for x number of days or
weeks. Nobody apart from that mother knows how
their child will be. The mother is the only person who
knows when it's right, when it's soon enough.

Louisa comes everywhere; that's been a condition
of me being able to do anything because she's not
ready for me to leave her overnight yet. When she is,
she'll be sleeping at my mum and dad's house first
because they live round the corner. We'll let the line
out and she can spread her wings when she's ready.
How you get to that point as an individual is down to
the child, what they're capable and ready to do; then
it's your situation and what you're able to arrange. I
arrange it so that Louisa's needs are put first.

SB: *It's refreshing to hear you talking about it in that way.*

SS: It should be the case that any woman in any job
should feel confident enough to speak up. If you
return to work and your boss says, 'You need to go
away for a conference in the States for a week', if
the mother's child isn't ready for that, if they've never

left them before, there has to be some negotiation. It can't just be 'maternity leave has finished'. It can't be like that. People have to be able to say, 'I can do this... and I can't do this.... My child isn't ready for me to leave her overnight.' Employers have to accept that and find a solution.

SB: *Culturally, some of Britain's employers are not ready. However the more of us that stand our ground and the more of us that say, 'I can't' or 'I won't', the better it makes life for those that follow.*

SS: I agree and I think we start to make it normal. I'm not saying take your children to work and let them run round the office. It's about being open. My child still needs me at night and that shouldn't be seen as a weakness. We seem obsessed in this country with babies sleeping alone for 12 hours a night as early as possible. If they can't, there's almost a stigma attached. You've failed, you've got them into a bad habit because they can't go to sleep without you. No – they're just not ready. We talk about self-soothing and how children do it. Their brains aren't ready until they're nearly four years old. We have to look at the facts and not some myth made up by someone who decided that children should be seen and not heard.

SB: *I've read that when Louisa was born, you started having contractions when you were on the turbo trainer.*

SS: I'd not felt like going out on the road. It was a lovely day. I live on the top of a hill so I used to take my bike in the car to a flatter part of Cheshire and ride in the lanes. I didn't feel right for doing it that day. It turns out because I was about to go into labour. I did a short session on the turbo in the garden. I thought I had Braxton Hicks but I ignored it. The next day we drove to Birmingham to pick up a new car and that following night they started a bit more.

Eventually I had a show and then I stopped feeling Louisa move. I went in to be monitored and it turned out I was three centimetres dilated. Unfortunately some gorilla of a midwife pumped me full of water saying I was dehydrated when I wasn't. That slowed my labour down; eventually Louisa got stuck and I ended up having an emergency C-section because she was getting distressed.

SB: *I hadn't realised you'd had a C-section – yet you were back training after six weeks?*

SS: Only because the six weeks was the minimum I was allowed, I had to rest… At first a couple of turbo sessions to make sure my stomach felt ok and then 45 minutes for the first ride on the road. Gradually I built it up over the following six weeks. I had another four weeks at home and then we went on my first training camp.

At first, I was training around Louisa. I'd be ready to go out on my bike as soon as she had a nap after a feed. If she seemed unsettled, I'd opt for the turbo so that I would be on hand in case she needed a feed again. If she seemed quite settled and in a deep sleep, I'd go out on my bike. Generally I wouldn't be out for longer than two hours at a time because she would not be able to go much longer than that between feeds.

When I went to training camp, I was doing two sessions a day to get the hours in. When we started back on the track for my first competition, it was a case of her being there so I could feed her if necessary. It was a matter of juggling. I was really lucky because my husband has a coaching business so he works from home and his work life is very flexible. That allows him to work when Louisa is asleep… we used a baby sling when she was tiny until about 14 months. That allowed her to sleep and hear your heartbeat, creating that concept of the fourth trimester.

We think she elongated that fourth trimester, liking to sleep in the sling with her dad. He would be doing his coaching on the laptop, stood at the breakfast bar while she slept. We found ways to make it work and keep her needs at the top of the list.

SB: *How does Barney find being a dad?*

SS: He's brilliant, he loves it. They have such a great relationship. She runs him ragged but they have this hilarious relationship; he makes her laugh and she's always giggling. Whenever I come back from a ride, they're waiting for me to have lunch or she's asleep on his shoulder. It's so lovely to see. When you're a couple and you talk about starting a family, you know your life will change but you don't have a concept of how.

The way that you are as parents impacts on how your life is as a family. Your reactions and your input to your child dictates the way that life is. You won't have a screaming baby if you recognise that your baby crying or making a noise means she's unhappy. It's a way for them to communicate that there's something they'd like you to help them with.

We've always had this philosophy that if she's crying there's a reason and we'll work out why to help her stop. Now we have a little girl who only cries when there's something wrong. She communicates to us and she knows we'll fix it quickly. That has been a revelation to us because we had no idea that would be the case.

Sarah went on to talk about how she met Barney...

SS: I was on a training camp as a swimmer and he was on the same training camp as a cyclist. You have multisport camps in the run up to the Olympic Games. The cycling team and the swim team chose to use that same camp in April 2004. He was with someone else at the time but by the following February he was single again. He turned up on my doorstep and asked me out for dinner. We've been together 10 years next month [February 2015]. He asked me to marry him after 11 months.

Talking about plans after Sarah retires from sport...

SS: One day I'd love to be the Chef de Mission of the team and lead the entire team of 22 sports to a Paralympic Games. I've told the BPA. Hopefully they'll help me pre-pare to have the skills that I need for the aspects that I haven't had the opportunity to experience as an athlete.

When you are an athlete, your body is your entire workforce and you have to look after it. Training comes first and sleep comes next. When you retire as a professional sportswoman, your purpose in life changes. It's going to be a completely different lifestyle and it will take some getting used to. I will no longer be able to use the excuse 'No I'm sorry my sleep's more important.'

I hope everything that you are doing helps to create more confident mums out there because it's an amazing journey. I feel privileged to have finally started this journey to being a mum.

The next interviews with Miriam McCaleb and then Dorothy Marlen provide some of the science behind Sarah's instinctive mothering.

Key learning points

1. You can do anything that you believe you can do.

2. Focus on what is most important for you and your child.

3. Trust in your instincts.

4. Mothers have a different role to fathers.

Additional resources

More information about Sarah's sporting success: www.teamstoreysport.com/sarah-storey.html.

How to nurture your child's brain development in the early years

Miriam McCaleb

She's a limbic creature. She's speaking German, I'm speaking Japanese. I have to meet her where she is. I have to get down on the floor.

Miriam McCaleb was part of a group that established the Brainwave Trust Aotearoa in the South Island, New Zealand in 2005. As well as having presented the Brainwave message more than a few times, she's worked as a university lecturer, an early childhood teacher and a parenting educator. These days she spends more time writing and parenting than teaching. Born in New Zealand, Miriam married an American and worked in the university system in Tennessee from 1999 to 2002. Later she moved back to New Zealand Brainwave Trust which is when she met the founder, Robin Fancourt, a paediatrician and colleague of Dr Bruce Perry. Miriam worked in education when From Neurons to Neighbourhoods and Rethinking The Brain were published.

SB: *Miriam, thank you so much for joining me. You started in education – how did you become so closely involved with the neuroscience and brain development community?*

MM: When psychiatrist Dr Bruce Perry came crashing into public consciousness, to me it was apparent that this new science was earth shattering. I naively thought, 'This is going to change everything because we now have irrefutable cellular evidence about the value of the first few years of a human's life; irrefutable unarguable evidence that early relationships are the most important; and that it is early in our lives that we need the most support and care.'

The most important thing in the world is to wrap ourselves as a society around families and the work of parenthood, the work of motherhood. I thought it meant we would no longer spend massive amounts of money on building prisons or fighting wars; we are going to invest in children because it's unarguable. It didn't work out like that.

MM: When we talk about development of the brain we are not just talking about someone who is going to do well at university. People hear 'development of the brain' and tend to think intelligence. That is only part of the story.

When we talk development of the brain, we are talking the whole person. When you decide what to cook for dinner, when you fall in love, when you drive your car, that's your brain at work. Every decision that we make and every thought that we have is generated by our brains.

Development of the brain is the development of emotional intelligence, and impulse control/self-regulation. Everybody wants the best for their babies and everybody hopes to provide something better than they had, whatever that may look or feel like. No one wants to make a mess of it.

We want our babies to have as many options as they can, to grow up feeling like they can make decisions for themselves and that they can do whatever they want in the world.

We are born with a brain exquisitely responsive to experience and not fully formed at birth. If you are a full term baby, all your organs are fully organised and functioning at birth; your heart is a miniature version of an adult heart, already pumping blood. That's not the case with the brain. It weighs about a third of its eventual adult weight and has significantly fewer brain cells. More to the point, the brain cells that are there are not synaptically connected.

When we have an experience, there is an electrical charge in the centre of the brain cell (called a neuron), which causes electrical charge activity to reach out. There is a little space in between the cells and the electrical charge leaps across the space; that's the synapse or the synaptic connection.

So if I am a baby and I cry, for example, mum picks me up and holds me close and comforts me, that's a lot of experiences wrapped into one. There's me the baby vocalising; there's the sound of mum's approach... let's call that one experience. I cried, I am comforted, I feel better. The first time I have that experience it takes a long time and a lot of work for my brain pathway to connect. It takes a long time for this cell to talk to this cell and create the pathway between. The more times I have a particular experience, or set of experiences, there's already a pathway between those two cells, and then that current can connect more readily and more quickly. Over time, that's important.

Here's the analogy that I like to use: we're neighbours and I'm going to your house. I have to walk through a jungle to get to your house. If I had a machete, the first time I go to your house, I have to work really hard to carve out a path, slice away the vines to get to your place through the jungle.

The next time I go to your house it's a bit easier. If I go to your house a lot of times, back and forth and back and forth, over time that's going to be easy for me to get to you. When I have a new experience, I'm going to have to use the machete and go in a different direction to carve a new pathway.

There are long-chain fatty acids present in human milk. Breast milk is perfectly mixed for creating and laying down myelin. Myelin is this fatty substance that is like the white plastic coating on a power cord. It allows the electric current to travel safely and without deviation, without losing any of its charge.

When a neural pathway is fully myelinated, the information can travel 250 times faster than when it is not fully myelinated. The brain decides which pathways to myelinate based around the frequency of a particular experience. If I am picked up and I am comforted most times when I cry, my brain myelinates a pathway that is doing huge amounts of work.

It tells me that the world is safe, I am worthy of comfort, my mother is a predictable and reliable figure in my life. This is wrapped up in that experience and the myelination of that experience. It's worth communicating my needs because someone is going to pick up on them.

If, occasionally, I cry and someone says, 'I have had it with you, I can't do any more,' that's not being myelinated the same way. All of us get a permission slip to occasionally be less than awesome. We are human beings and we are fallible. Aspiring for perfection in motherhood is unhelpful. It's a disservice.

As a baby, the more times we have an experience, the stronger the pathway becomes. When we're fully myelinated, we have very efficient pathways in the brain. This is significant because around the age of three, we prune away about 40% of the brain cells we were born with. The ones we keep, are the ones that are involved in the synapses we use most often.

MM: When you aspire for perfection in your motherhood, you have a mental image of how things should go. Immediately you're engaged in a struggle when things don't go the way you want; now your energy is spent trying to make things how you want them to be, instead of responding to what's right in front of you. Trying to be perfect is harmful. It's hard for those of us who strive to make As and A+s. I aim for a C in my mothering, because it gives me permission to respond to what's happening in front of me and the interactive sloppiness of real life.

We don't have perfect interactions with amazingly scripted children. We have mucky faced challenges thrown across our paths all the time. You can spend your energy rolling with it or spend your energy making it a vision of perfect.

Going back to the brain development... Bruce Perry's neuro-sequential model[1] explains the brain by imagining a layer cake. This model helps to explain what toddlers are going through and why they have such a hard time.

The first layer of the brain that develops is the **brain stem**. The stem of your brain controls your autonomic systems: blood temperature, blood pressure, body temperature, heart rate, blinking, food digestion etc. These are in place when we are first born.

What a baby needs the most during those early days is calm, safety, consistency and predictability. This is the more primitive region of our brain, the bit that we have in common with reptiles. It is housed at the base of your brain at the top of your spine. It controls our freeze or flight response. When we are in danger, this is where we downshift to.

---

[1] *Applying Principles of Neurodevelopment to Clinical Work with Maltreated and Traumatized Children,* 2006. http://childtrauma.org/wp-content/uploads/2013/08/Perry-Bruce-neurosequentialmodel_06.pdf

When we are first born, our brain stem is in charge. We don't want to myelinate lots of pathways around activation of fight or flight. Contrary to what some people might think, this is powerful. The younger the baby, the more imprint the early experiences have because of the myelination process.

Babies get what they need through loving arms, warm chest, predictable adults, as few adults as possible so that they can form attachments one at a time.

The next layer is the **midbrain**. This is predominantly the home of the motor regions. You know when babies are getting into this stage. It used to be that in your arms is the best place in the world. Babies hit that point when they're really interested in moving and particularly moving away. They are harder to hold and they may be not so engaged at the breast, they're looking around.

That's a good cue that the baby is wiring up the midbrain, when they become really interested and motivated by movement. The best thing we can do is to support children in moving as much as possible. Allow them to explore the full, free range of natural movement. Pay attention to how often your baby is able to kick and stretch on the floor, how often your baby is held. When babies are held, we tend to move with them but if babies spend lots of time in walker trainers, high chairs, strollers, they can't get in or out by themselves.

Remember good enough is good enough. If you have a baby in a bouncy seat so you can get dinner on the table for the rest of the family, no problem.

It gets exciting after that. We've learned to hold up our baby head and we've rocked on hands and feet. We've rolled over, we've crawled, we've pulled up to stand, and we've started walking. We are, by definition, a toddler. That's when the 'terrible twos' malarkey starts. This is the development of our **limbic system**, our emotional brain (sometimes called the mammalian brain).

Our limbic system is the home of our emotions. It's important to recognise that with toddlers, they learn to feel stuff long before they learn how to control what it is that they're feeling.

The last layer that comes online is our **cortex**. This is the big juicy bit of our brain. Our cortex teaches us to use computers, write code, have higher analytical thought, and create art. Arguably the most important function of our cortex is that it regulates our limbic system.

If I'm angry and I want to punch somebody, my cortex jumps in: 'You know what, that's not going to be terribly helpful, there are some negative implications here, let's think it through, you've got options.' The cortex does that analytical thinking.

Toddlers are developing their limbic system; you cannot rush them into this rational way of thinking. They are not there yet.

The best way to parent a toddler deep in their limbic system is to meet them where they are. I'll give you an example. When my oldest daughter was a toddler we made juice pops. I was a more diligent mother with limiting sugar with my first child. I'm sure everybody recognises that.

I made up juice pops: fruit juice and water, and you freeze it. They come with different coloured sticks. She was going through that pink phase. 'Can I please have the pink one?' 'I'm sorry honey, there's not a pink one. I've got blue, green, yellow, which would you like?' 'I want the pink one.' 'I'm sorry honey, I don't have the pink. I've got blue, green, or yellow.' She is upset and collapses on the floor in a fit of distress.

Babies and young children are capable of feeling deep emotion but they're not capable yet of understanding, 'This emotion will pass.' Adults have the accumulated experience to have an expectation, 'I feel lousy but I'm confident I'm going to feel better later.' Toddlers don't have that. They have 'right here, right now'.

They are our teachers of how to be present and mindful. They are masters of it. Adults want to rush in with logic, 'But honey the pink one is exactly the same as the yellow one, the green and the blue, it's the same juice.' That's a logical message, a message of the cortex and she's a limbic creature. She's speaking German, I'm speaking Japanese. I have to meet her where she is. I have to get down on the floor and say, 'I see. It looks like you are disappointed. It's hard when you can't have what you want, isn't it?' I don't have to share what she is feeling. Secretly, I might be thinking, 'For goodness sake, it's just a juice pop,' but I don't express that. That would be cruel and belittle her emotional experience.

Being willing to feel stuff alongside our kids makes a lot of us uncomfortable. Many of us weren't parented that way ourselves. We live in a culture obsessed with feeling good and suppressing the negative feelings. I don't believe there are 'negative' feelings; there are emotions. This is this emotion. I feel you and I label you. I accept what it feels like to be sad or angry or disappointed. I breathe with you and I let you pass and then you'll pass.

Children need practice with that and they need a wise guide to walk alongside them. Sometimes our kids drive us nuts and it's hard to do. I hope that I've given my child time in the first instance to sit alongside her, and say, 'I can see that you're sad and that's ok. It's ok to be disappointed when things don't go our way, because that's a normal, natural, human reaction.'

Excitement is another emotion that I notice parents downplay. Children's excitement can be unsettling, in the same way as their anger.

We don't know what jealousy is when we're 18 months old, or that frustration is different to anger.

SB: *What if we don't get it right in those first couple of years, have we ruined our children for life?*

MM: Change is always possible. It's like building a house. You can go back into a house and do remedial foundation work. It is possible to create change but it takes time, patience, wisdom and skill on the part of the adults. I lean here on the work of Bruce Perry. He works with children who have had a difficult start to their lives.

His first book was *The Boy Who Was Raised as a Dog*. He reminds us that we need to meet children where they are in terms of this process and start there. If that means I'm meeting somebody who needs support and development of brain stem, midbrain, or reptilian brain, I need to go back to there.

Something I found liberating came from the work of Dr Daniel Siegel who is a brain scientist. He coined the term 'rupture and repair'. He talks about the damaging effects of stress hormones on the developing brain; he shares how those damaging effects are largely mitigated by comfort and care.

The time that you lose it – for example, if I thought you were asleep and I left you to have a nap while I put the groceries away. If unbeknownst to me you've woken up and you're a blithering wreck, and you're crying. Oh no, that brain lady told me that too much stress in the developing brain is corrosive and damaging. I've ruined my kid forever and I'm feeling really guilty. I rush to pick you up and you won't calm down, then I get so irate that I scream at you: 'Just stop crying, I didn't mean to!' Then I'm feeling even worse about myself as a mother…

Daniel Siegel tells us that unpleasantness is rupture. We can repair that by going to our child with an open, soft heart and saying, 'Honey, I am sorry. Now I'm just going to hold you while you cry. I don't have to fix it. I don't have to change it. I'm going to be a warm safe place for you to let that out.'

Our babies will regulate themselves according to what we're doing. Our heart rate influences their heart rate; our breathing pattern influences their breathing pattern. If we're stressed and tense, we can't provide comfort. Rule number one, always comfort thyself. I pretend to empty the compost, whether I'm emptying the compost or not, so I can get outside and do ten big deep breaths by myself before I come in and tackle whatever is happening in the house.

Rupture and repair; take real comfort that after any episode that you felt ended badly, if you follow up with, 'I'm sorry, can I give you a cuddle,' you've repaired what has gone wrong before. What is clear from the research is that there are risk factors and resilience factors in the life of children. The resilience factors take you forward, for example secure relationships with parents, living in one place, not too many changes, breastfeeding etc.

There are certain things that are not so helpful: such as smoking during pregnancy, family violence or lots of partners coming through mum's life. On their own, those things are not terrible. If mum is breastfeeding, she wears you in a sling and she has a bunch of boyfriends, you're ahead of the game.

Accept that there are risk factors and there are resilience factors and do your best.

Families need to take heart that everyone's landscape looks different. We've experienced real trauma and grief in the loss of our city [Christchurch earthquake], and I lost my mum while my youngest was a tiny baby; I was something of a basket case for a few months. Risk factor. I was breastfeeding, resilience factor. We all have our own stories. No-one gets a fairytale; our kids don't get fairytales. We are preparing them for life in an imperfect world.

What I've noticed lately is the invisibility of motherhood. Not just the raising babies, but the keeping of the castle, the laundry, cooking the meals, cleaning the toilets, the vast majority of motherhood is invisible. As a mum, I've been feeling the invisibility of that. What I'm working to do in my world, and what I ask of all mums is to notice each other. Notice the work that only we are going to recognise.

Naomi Stadlen recently published *How Mothers Love*. It's one of those examples of the millions of ways that we demonstrate our love every day. Invisible. It's lovely when we notice those things for each other. The only people who are going to notice and comment are other mums. I'm working hard to do that in my own life, to notice my friends and other mums and the work that they do. It will give you strength in those moments when you feel, 'I'm just beating my head.' No, you're not. Someone's noticing. We notice.

In the next interview with Dorothy Marlen, Dorothy explores further how we continue to build the attachment with our young children through respectful bodily care.

Key learning points

1. What a baby needs the most during those early days is calm, safety, consistency and predictability.

2. Toddlers feel deep emotion but they are not yet capable of rationalisation.

3. There are risk factors and there are resilience factors.

4. Good enough is good enough.

5. Note the invisibility of motherhood and notice what we as mums do.

Additional resources

Brainwave Trust, a not-for-profit organisation whose aim is to spread awareness and educate the New Zealand community about the latest scientific research about early brain development: www.brainwave.org.nz/

Learn more about Miriam's work at www.baby.geek.nz.

Gentle parenting allows the child to develop in her own time

Dorothy Marlen

[When] there is a predictability, the child is happier, calmer and less stressed.

Dorothy Marlen is an Early Childhood Consultant and Trainer. When Dorothy was a mother herself, she came across the Steiner way of education. She was the first person from the UK to train at the Pikler Institute. She now runs workshops for parents, and parent and child groups to support the early years, using the Steiner and Pikler approaches. She believes it is crucial that we bring the fullest awareness, love and respect into our care of the very young child. Dorothy starts by explaining her influences: Rudolf Steiner and Emmi Pikler.

DM: Rudolf Steiner was an educationist in the last century. He developed a way of education that honoured the unfolding that every child goes through over the first 21 years. This gave me an overview and a context for parenting. For me it made it so much easier because I could see what was appropriate and what wasn't at different ages of the child. With schooling in this country we are forced to try and get the fruit from the child before they've had a chance to grow. Steiner helped me to see the more subtle aspects of child development, not just the intellectual but the emotional and the spiritual aspects.

Emmi Pikler was a paediatrician in Hungary and her genius was to see how to give respectful care to the young child. She realised that if we didn't interfere with a young child's motor development, the child would come up into standing without our interference. And they'd be much stronger and more competent for that. She first put this into her own paediatric practice with families in Budapest and then in an orphanage that she set up after the war. The children came out of that orphanage as healthy children, emotionally and physically.

What I learnt at the Pikler Institute has profoundly woken me up to what we culturally do to children without even realising it. I learned that we can give more respectful care. We can build that attachment and bonding during times of bodily care. Yet those are usually the times when we rush – for example we rush through nappy changes. The Pikler approach turns that around to slow down and create times of joyful co-operation which creates a very secure attachment with the child. It forms a security within the child which can unfold through childhood. I feel it gets to the nub of what attachment is and how we can make parenting simpler.

DM: For example when you're breastfeeding a child, be absolutely present to what is happening, not on the end of your mobile phone or on the computer. By being absolutely present, you're filling that child with love and a sense of security. Changing the nappy happens several times a day over three years. It means being present and doing the bodily care task with the child and not to it, creating a cooperative endeavour.

It becomes a different sort of experience than doing it 'to' the child. It's a time when you can build attachment and bonding. These things are respectful and the child responds. It's filling them up with your presence and your love. From that base they are happy to begin to explore the environment around them.

It's different from rushing through these things and maybe giving half attention because we're busy doing other things. Slow down and give your full presence to the child, particularly during these very intimate moments of care, and you build a deeply secure core in the child.

Sometimes with attachment parenting we think we need to be with the child, entertaining the child all the time, especially when they're very small. It's exhausting for everybody but balance it with times when you can put the baby on their back, let them move freely and you don't need to be entertaining them all the time.

As adults we need both; we need times of intimacy and love with a special person and we need times of freedom. Even a baby needs this. I don't mean abandoning them and going out of the room but just putting them down, being close by, sitting back and observing the amazing things that they can do. They can go into rolling, into crawling, into sitting, into standing without us having to help them. That's a great relief to know that we don't have to do that; the child has that wisdom in them, it's there already. And the child is more confident for being allowed to have that freedom.

There's a generation of children growing up with parents who use a lot of technology and who have felt that their parents weren't there for them. You don't have to be there all the time but have those secure moments through the day where the child knows that they're going to have the full presence of their parent or carer.

DM: Nobody's to blame – we're waking up and seeing what the cultural conditioning is. We're beginning to realise through neuroscience and attachment theory that we can wake up more and practise being present. We're having to learn how to be more present in everything, not just with our children but with other people in the world. It's evolutionary.

DM: Pennie Brownlee, a New Zealander, does a lot of work with carers out of the Pikler approach as well. She says there's a *biological imperative*, how children, how human beings need to be, to grow up healthy: what they need in their environment and from the carers around them. Then there's the *cultural imperative* which is what's going on culturally. In the West, those two don't match. What the child needs, particularly in the early months and years, is out of kilter with what we're being given culturally.

It's a very difficult time to be a parent because there are so many different pressures, options and alternatives. My way through this maze was to get a spiritual perspective which helped me to see the bigger picture of child development. This is what Rudolf Steiner gave me. The Pikler approach helped me to see what respectful care looked like in practice.

DM: It's so simple but so profound because you want your child to feel secure in what is happening. The main way they feel secure is if things happen in the same way again and again and again. The repetition makes them feel secure. When they're secure, they feel happy and they can play; they're relaxed and calm.

I would hate to live in a world where I didn't have any control over what was going on. But we regularly do this with children and don't even think about it. We suddenly pick them up, we take them here, we take them there, they wake up in somebody's house and then in somebody else's house. It puts a lot of stress into them which doesn't help them to sleep at night or doesn't help with feeding.

The more rhythm and predictability that a very young child has in their life, the happier they are and the easier it is in the end for the parents.

DM: For example, do the bedtime routine in the same order every night. The child feels a deep security. The Steiner piece is about having a predictable rhythm in the day; a mixture of what we call breathing out and breathing in. Active times and calm times. What can happen easily is we have one active time after another, after another, with no calm times in between.

During the day have periods of activity and periods of calm: a calm breakfast, then an active period; calm time round the snack and then more active, then calm time and a nap at lunch time and so on. There is a predictability and the child is happier, calmer and less stressed. It's old fashioned really, it's the sort of thing that we used to do.

It goes back to this biological imperative of the young child. The child needs rhythm and this 'breathing' during the day. If we ignore that, the child will become more and more unhappy and distressed.

It's good to have patterns all through childhood even if it's just an anchoring at mealtimes, everybody's sitting round the table at lunchtime and suppertime.

There are three phases of childhood:

0 to 7, the child is growing and developing a strong constitution for life; she is learning how to play and be creative. Good rhythm helps. At Steiner Kindergartens the children know what's going to happen and there is lots of time for play. The children breathe not just with their lungs but their whole being breathes.

7 to 14, the middle time of childhood, there's a big change around the age of seven – we think that the dropping out of the milk teeth is an arbitrary thing. But at some more subtle energetic level, it's showing that the child is moving from one phase of childhood

into another. At six, they're ready for formal learning. We have this big debate in this country about when children are ready to read and write. Naturally, children are ready to have formal learning when they're six or seven like on the continent. This is a biological imperative of a young child.

From 14, puberty is another marker of huge changes in the child. The child is ready for intellectual input. Our parenting styles have to change enormously to accommodate the teenager.

The child is changing all the way through childhood. A totally different child emerges in the second seven years of life and in the teenage years. Knowing that makes parenting much easier because we know what's appropriate, and what isn't.

We might have to put away the technology as much as possible while we have young children, but that stage does not last forever. We can find ways of using our adult technology when little children aren't around.

DM: Culturally and in parenting, it's moving so fast and yet the biological imperative of a young child doesn't change; nature doesn't change. We need to be aware of that. What I've found helpful is the spiritual understanding of the young child, knowing the three phases of childhood, knowing that rhythm is important, and knowing how to give respectful care. I wish I'd known more of this when I was raising my son.

SB: *If our children aren't ready for formal learning until they're six, yet in this country, they start school much earlier, how does that manifest itself?*

DM: In various ways. One is that children fail their five-year-old tests. It's not because they haven't been started early enough, it's because they're not ready, as simple as that. My son went to a Steiner school and he learnt to read at seven and it was so easy. There was no struggle and he loves reading. That's the difference. Some children want to read at four, that's fine, but the majority aren't ready. At the change of teeth, this subtle change in them happens and they are emotionally ready for this next learning time.

If a child's forced to do something that they're not ready for, they lose confidence in themselves and their ability. It can affect their learning journey all the way through.

Richard House [freelance educational consultant and campaigner] has written a lot about this. He and other early childhood educationists are trying to put pressure on the government to change their policies. Another example is that we sit up our children very early at five months old so that they're ready for baby-led weaning. Which means that they often don't go through the crawling stage. It gets missed because they're sat up too early. If crawling does not happen this may affect the integration of primitive reflexes in the first year of life, which may cause problems with learning in school. That can affect how easily a child can learn to read and write. Many disruptive elements in classrooms are not because a child wants to be naughty but because they've got retained reflexes that make it difficult for them to sit still and focus. They might be too young as well.

A child needs to crawl before sitting up. Sally Goddard-Blythe works in schools helping them to work with children with retained reflexes.

There's a huge range in how children reach the milestones and go through those phases. Some babies will sit up very early, four or five months. Others might lay on their backs until they're eight months old. There's a huge range and the more we can step back and allow this unfolding movement to happen itself, the more deeply confident children are in their bodies. And the more satisfying it is for parents because they can begin to trust their child's wisdom.

You can't teach a young child anything, up to seven they have to find it all themselves; they have to experience it themselves. Children want to imitate people and they want to play outside. There is this pressure to get children to sit up by six months so they can be baby-led weaned. I think that the sitting up too early stops the crawling and then we have other problems down the line.

Once the child comes up into standing, they begin to talk. The whole thing comes together once the child is upright and we don't have to do anything apart from speak well in their presence. Speak to them simply using the human voice, singing songs or nursery rhymes. Technology doesn't work to help voice or speech. It happens naturally if we talk to them, share things with them, explain what we're doing to them. Not overwhelming with intellectual chat but ordinary day-to-day conversation. Their speech will come naturally.

Every child is totally individual. Each child goes through the same archetype, through the same stages. One stage builds on the other but each child is totally individual.

DM: Unfortunately with the developmental charts that we have now, we forget that each child is individual. They are their own selves and they come with their own destiny, their own gifts and their own challenges. The Pikler approach is about being there present for your child and observing them so you get to know who this little person is: their quirks, what makes them happy, what makes them sad.

A child's biological imperative is that they need somebody to care for them because they're unable to. They're powerless. They find ways to engage the parent or their carers. If it's a difficult situation where the mother's depressed and doesn't respond, the child may begin to give up and won't try so hard.

If it's a cooperative partnership with your child, you can avoid the power thing that kicks in around toddlerhood. If you have a partnership rather than a power dynamic, things are easier.

Simple toys make active children. I would ban things like Bumbo seats and baby bouncers, because the children become very passive. It's much better if they're allowed to have a lot of movement, time for free movement and simple toys, often the things you can find in your kitchen.

SB: *An important point around this cultural conditioning; it's not that we're doing things badly or inappropriately for any reason other than we've been culturally conditioned.*

DM: Yes, it's the way we were brought up, it's what we see all around us. We make assumptions that it's alright to stick a hat on a baby's head without telling it what we're doing. Or we might change a nappy without even looking at the child. Being taken round a big shopping mall with the buggy facing outwards is probably very stressful for the child. If we can see the world through their eyes, that can help the child not to get overstimulated and stressed.

SB: *It's the cultural conditioning and trying to see the world through our children's eyes. That in itself can be so powerful and we need to be reminded to do that more often.*

Key learning points

1. See the world through your children's eyes.

2. Young children benefit from respectful bodily care.

3. The more rhythm and predictability that a very

young child has, the happier they are and the easier it is for the parents.

4. As parents we need to be aware of and respond to our children's real needs and wake up to where these may be at odds with the cultural lifestyles we take for granted.

Additional resources

International Emmi Pikler Foundation: http://pikler.org.

Steiner Waldorf Schools Fellowship: www.steinerwaldorf. org/.

How to build emotional wellbeing through self-love

Toni Brodelle

One of the greatest services that we do for each other as mums, is when we're present to each other. We don't try and provide solutions, we're just here with each other; when it's tough we're there.

Toni Brodelle is the founder of Incredible Me, the home of emotional wellbeing and global empowerment for inspirational young people and their amazing grown ups. Toni started working in education and from that became very aware of the emotional wellbeing needs of the children she worked with. She developed Incredible Me after running a project which worked holistically with families of children considered to be at risk of exclusion from school. Toni is also on the board of directors for a global organisation, the Pay It Forward Foundation.

TB: As mums we put ourselves under a lot of pressure. I think it's time that we support one another and support ourselves so we can help our children and help our world become a better place. I'm passionate about our world becoming a kinder place. That can't happen until we're kinder to ourselves. I believe women, and specifically mothers, have a huge role to play in moving our world to a better place. When

I talk about mothers nurturing their own wellbeing, I see the ramifications globally.

When I trained as a teacher, I was drawn to working with children who needed help with their emotional wellbeing; it's the foundation for everything. If children can access robust emotional wellbeing, they can access anything. If you can teach them to believe in themselves and to be resilient when it comes to challenges, they'll try – and trying is the heart of learning.

Emotional wellbeing is about how we think and feel about ourselves; how we use that to make a positive impact in our lives; how we shape our lives positively. The better we think and feel about ourselves, the more positive our lives are likely to be.

Self-esteem is a part of emotional wellbeing. However there is also emotional resilience which is about how we encounter roadblocks in our lives and how we deal with those.

SB: *As a mother, if I don't have strong emotional wellbeing, what's the likely impact on my children?*

TB: We know that children pick up from what we do far more than from what we say. Our children are watching us and if we're not looking after ourselves we're teaching them. This was perhaps the strongest motivator for me when I started along this path. I'll be completely honest – I didn't grow up with parents who knew how to nurture their emotional wellbeing. It was new for me. What motivated me was that if I didn't learn, my children would learn from what I did.

Aside from the responsibility we have for ourselves, it's understanding that our children are shaped by what we do. We're teaching simple things. For example I've always had 'pockets of time' through the day that are sacrosanct for me. I'm absolutely present with my children for the vast majority of the time but there are times that my children know are sacrosanct and unless somebody is hurt or at risk or the house is burning, it can wait two minutes. If I'm having a shower or if I'm getting dressed or if I've gone into my bedroom and shut the door, that's when I'm taking five minutes out.

For a while, I wondered, am I excluding my children? As mothers we question ourselves. I then realised that I was modelling that for my children. Now my children do it. My eldest daughter is 11 and she will take herself off: 'I need some time.' For me it's positive to see that she's looking after her emotional wellbeing. My youngest daughter will do the same, albeit to a lesser degree.

As mothers we need to be mindful that we are shaping our children with whatever we do. We choose how that shaping happens, whether it's through an empowering or less empowering way.

Nurturing your emotional wellbeing will be different for everybody. We have different things that make us tick. For me it's a case of having time to myself and shutting off outside distractions. For other people it might be to go for a run or play music. The first element is knowing what makes you tick.

Identify the times you've felt most connected to yourself and felt most at ease. I love spending time cooking. It's very therapeutic for me. I've felt most connected to myself in my kitchen cooking. Connect to yourself and understand those times that you feel at peace and go to that place when you need it.

As mothers we tend to absorb everybody's needs. It's important that we learn to prioritise our own needs to be able to give more to other people. To do that, we really have to know ourselves.

SB: *I first starting running on a caravan holiday. The weather had been miserable so we'd been indoors all day. I found it difficult to cope, being in a small space with no silence. I thought, 'I've just got to get out of this caravan. I don't care that it's pouring with rain.' Now running is that place I go when I need it.*

TB: I think that's one of the greatest services that we do for each other as mums, is when we're present to each other. We don't try and provide solutions, we're just here with each other; when it's tough we're there. We're all just doing the best we can. It's not about being perfect, it is about being good enough.

Sometimes being good enough is shutting yourself in the bathroom to get five minutes of peace so that when you come out you can be the best mum that you can be. Or going for a run so that you get that headspace. I'm betting Sherry that if you'd stayed in the caravan you'd have been more fractious and a lot less fun for your family to be around.

TB: I think this is something that for too long we haven't been aware of. We've allowed ourselves as women and mothers to be devalued in some ways. We have a huge role to play as mothers. Not just in the lives of our children but thinking of the events of the last week and what happened in Paris [Gunmen attacked the Paris office of the French satirical magazine, *Charlie Hebdo*, killing 12].

Part of Incredible Me is about global empowerment. It's about shaping yourself in a positive way to make a positive impact on the world. I'm passionate about moving our world to a better place. As mothers, we are in the optimal position to shape the future by giving our children strong roots to grow and wings to fly. As mums we give and give and give and give. One of the most rewarding things about being a mum is that you're able to do that, but we can't keep giving unless we're also replenishing the tank.

The more that we do that, the more we can create. If we take time to look after our emotional wellbeing, we can nurture children with strong emotional wellbeing. We raise children with a strong sense of self and a strong sense of loving themselves, who are therefore more open and able to love other people.

Women will walk into a room and will take in the whole thing. They ask themselves, 'Where do I fit into this?' We absorb everyone else's energy and dynamics – we do that in families too. Men tend to be more in their own space. It doesn't mean they're not open to those dynamics but they're not necessarily relating to them in the same way.

It creates a bit of a bubble where men are more able to compartmentalise what they are doing and less likely to feel bombarded or overwhelmed. They tend to have one focus at a time. They don't tend to get that sense of a multitude of needs bombarding them. Which possibly makes it easier for them to nurture their own emotional wellbeing.

In parenting, much depends on the dynamics within the family. I've known families where the dad is the stay-at-home main care giver. Often then the dynamic is reversed and you do have a dad who feels bombarded and absorbs everybody's needs. I think it's more about the family dynamic and culture. If you've grown up with parents who had a propensity to look after their own emotional wellbeing, they're more likely to have fostered that within you.

SB: *How do we tackle the emotional wellbeing of children?*

TB: It's understanding that all behaviour is communication whether we're talking about children or adults. We're communicating the best way we know, given the means we have at that time. It's understanding the need that underlies the communication. We support the children and parents to meet that need in a more empowering way.

For example, you might have children lashing out because they didn't have the communication skills to make their needs known. They are communicating through their behaviour rather than through words. Often people will interpret those behaviours in very different ways, especially in a school setting. It's about equipping the children with the communication skills.

Sometimes you see a child almost acting out at school. It might be a child who is bullied. When working with that child, it becomes apparent that it's a learned behaviour. Perhaps there are parental pressures or a breakdown in parental communication. There might be a need for emotional wellbeing work with the parents to deal with the problem at its core.

We all need these skills. Even people who have grown up with a robust family setting that encouraged emotional wellbeing. We all have challenges and it's about keeping that at the front of our minds. Making sure that we are fostering our own emotional wellbeing and constantly revisiting it. Not just assuming it's a done deal.

It is about looking at the communication and putting the skills in place, empowering people to find the support that's necessary to deal with the problem at its cause.

SB: *My parents split up when I was a teenager and inevitably that had an impact on my own emotional wellbeing. If you've been through a difficult experience in childhood, what can you do to nurture yourself?*

TB: There is a supposed textbook pattern of emotional development that we all go through. We learn emotional skills at different life stages. For example we learn attachment early on.

If we go through a life trauma – a family breakdown, grief, a major move – our emotional development in that area is interrupted. The child might stay stuck at that point until they revisit it and work on that area.

You might see adults revert to a chronologically young behaviour when it comes to saying goodbye, for example when moving jobs or at the end of a relationship. The key is to go back and give space for the healing of that memory. Feeling the things yourself that perhaps you wanted somebody else to be when you were younger. The love from other people is always more fragile because it can be taken away. Love that comes from ourselves *to* ourselves is very robust because only you decide to take that away.

It's almost like giving ourselves permission to leave it in the past. Not feeling that we have to carry it with us, not having to relive it over and over again.

When I was growing up, my mother was very abusive. I had a fear that I would be that mother. For me the healing was not just healing what had happened in the past but allowing myself to be free of it. Where I've been, does not have to be where I am going. I can be free and I can be the mother that I choose to be, by creating who and what that will look like.

At the same time, everything that I've been through has shaped me positively and in a strong way. I do not want to leave that part behind. It's letting go of the pain and bringing forward the strength.

SB: *I have an inner strength and confidence which I believe comes from the grief and trauma that I experienced in my teenage years. It's made me tough and strong. I wouldn't necessarily wish other people to go through the same experiences, however I believe I have a strength that maybe I wouldn't have had otherwise.*

TB: Everything that I've gone through growing up has given me a degree of empathy that I wouldn't have had otherwise. I realised that I'm only going to be that kind of mother if I choose to be that kind of mother. From here on, I define what I want that to look like.

You set your stall out as a parent. You choose what is non-negotiable for you. It might be that, for you, it's imperative that you are at every school assembly and at the school gates. It might be that it's important that you set a strong model of what being a working mum looks like. It's personal to you. Beyond that things are negotiable.

I developed an understanding that my mum didn't know how to be otherwise. For me, it was learning how to talk about my feelings and talking about them with my children, allowing myself to be vulnerable. Giving them space to be vulnerable, not expecting perfection.

There were a lot of things that I took consciously from my childhood. It was an empowering experience to look back and ask, 'What am I choosing?' instead of just dragging this big bag with me. Choosing what I'm going to carry with me into my parenting and into my professional life.

SB: *How will I know if my child does not have a strong emotional wellbeing?*

TB: There will be many signs. It would depend on you and your child. We know that feeling we have as parents when we feel out of sorts, everything's getting to us and we're reacting to things with a shorter fuse. Our children are the same.

It might be the acting-out behaviours with our children. Are they bored? Are they irritating each other? Are they arguing over silly things? Are we noticing that they're fractious at particular times of the day? It's about pattern spotting and having in your mind that all behaviour is communication. It's not behaviour for behaviour's sake. Whether it's boredom, unhappiness… it's looking for the messages behind the behaviour.

SB: *Such a powerful concept. If you understand that all behaviour is communication, you appreciate that people aren't being angry or moody for the sake of being angry or moody. There's something underneath.*

TB: It's so liberating because then you come from a place of listening and not being defensive. The times when you say something without really saying it and then stop yourself. Catching yourself and asking, 'What am I communicating with my behaviour? Is there a better way? Do I have words to communicate this?'

SB: *Sometimes as mothers we tend to jump into situations to try to solve the problem when perhaps your child just needs space.*

TB: One of the most important things that you can do when something is happening is ask your child if they're ready to talk. If there is adrenalin coursing around their body, that adrenalin can shut off their higher thinking capacity. Ask 'Are you ready to speak, do you need some time?'

It's easier for parents to go into ego and to think, 'I have to assert myself here.' It's being more conscious and remembering what the goal is. The goal is communication, resolution and reparation. We both have to be in a place where we're ready to work to that aim. The child or the young person has to be open to that as much as we do.

As parents, it's easy to lump our children together especially when we're trying to fulfil so many needs. Understand that those children are individuals. They're growing on their own path, not our path, and we are there to give them the roots that they need to grow and the wings to fly. Some of the most important work we do as mothers is fostering that independence, not stepping in.

It's natural to feel protective and to want to guide our children. Nobody prepares you for the second child being so different and the demands being so different. As a mother, step back and observe them. Observe and get to know your children as you would anybody. Allow them to find that space, to find the person that they are and allow that process to develop. We don't have to be woven throughout it but be there walking alongside them, watching the process naturally unfold. Guiding them as best suits them.

One of the joys of being a parent is getting to know your own children. We have this delusion as parents that we're expected to know our children. We only ever really know them in hindsight. Give yourself permission as a parent to be open to that. Be open to getting to know yourself and getting to know your children every day.

You can get to know yourself by being self-aware. It means that you have to clear space: physical and emotional space. Even if it is just five minutes. Understanding, how did I react to that situation? Was that different to how I've reacted in the past? Reflect on how we're creating our worlds, being mindful of it. It's being present in the moment and being aware of what we're doing, doing what we're doing mindfully. It's the understanding that we're growing and learning until we die. It's about having a growth mindset rather than a fixed mindset.

The growth mindset is so much more powerful because it allows you to change and develop; to recognise that you don't know all the answers. As mothers we never will know all the answers.

One of the greatest gifts we can give to our children is the understanding that we're always growing, we're always learning. That I don't have all of the answers and that's ok. It can be damaging for children if we come from a place of having all the answers; it can make them feel less for not having all the answers.

Carol Dweck did amazing research on children who were given a task to do. Some of the children were praised based on their character, 'You finished so you must be really smart.' Other children were praised based on their efforts and the process, 'You've finished that, that's brilliant, you're trying really hard, you're learning.'

At the time both groups responded equally positively to the praise. What was interesting is that when the children were given their next more challenging task, where there was a risk of them not succeeding instantly, the children who were praised based on their character were more reluctant to try because they had a fear of losing that.

Whereas the children who had been praised based on their effort, using more growth mindset language, were more open to taking the risk. They understood that part of the process is you're going to fall down. You fall down seven times, get up eight, and they had a real understanding of that.

As mothers, we have to model that for our children. We have to use that language to ourselves and with them, we have to be forgiving of ourselves and to understand that we're in progress the whole time. Everything is a process and that's powerful for children.

SB: *As a child I was told I was clever; and I didn't want to try things if I thought I might fail. I guess I thought it might prove that I wasn't clever after all.*

TB: Because it's so closely tied to your identity rather than your effort. Identity is more fixed whereas effort is more movable. We've all had times where we've chosen not to make effort. We have that within our control whereas our identity is outside of our control, especially if it's externally validated in that way.

SB: *That is the most valuable thing to take away – praise the process and the effort. I understand now why, in the past, I have steered away from things if I thought I might not be successful. I didn't want to be seen to fail.*

TB: What we get praised for creates our emotional roadmap.

SB: *As children we want the attention of our parents and if you get attention by being clever, you to want to carry on doing that.*

TB: This applies to everybody. As human beings our only real emotional need is to be loved. Every fear that we have boils down to, 'I'm not enough and I think if I'm not enough, I won't be loved.' From very early on, our emotional blueprint is around, 'How do I get love?'

Two questions that you can ask that help you to understand how your emotional blueprint has been shaped:

- When you were younger, whose love did you crave the most? Answer instinctively, don't think about it.

- In order to have to experience that love, what did I have to do and who did I have to be? Love could be respect, praise, appreciation, time... love comes in many forms.

I knew that my dad loved me but I also knew that he was supremely proud of me when I achieved academically. That created a child who wanted to do well academically. It also created a child who was afraid of not doing well academically. I did exceptionally well at school but always stopped short of what I could have achieved; I didn't want to risk that failure. Failure meant losing love.

It's not about being perfect, it's about being good enough. It's about being mindful, knowing ourselves and loving ourselves where we're at right now.

When do you give your children time? When do you give them praise? What do they get praised for? Being kind? Getting good grades in school? What do you give them visible affection for? We express love in different ways, when do we show them that love? What's the pattern? That pattern will usually tie into our own experiences because we give love in the way that we like to receive it. It is usually the way we have received it in the past.

SB: *I am aware of my need to be good at everything. I don't want to pass that 'need' onto my daughters. I don't want them to think that I'll only love them if they have good grades at school.*

TB: That's where the fixed and growth mindsets are important; praise them for trying, not succeeding. Praise them for doing things outside their comfort zone. For doing things which are silly and fun and gratuitously not academic. All of those are important but it's the language that we use and being forgiving of ourselves and of them.

Brené Brown talks about being in the arena with dust on your face. As parents, it's about getting in there, showing ourselves falling over and laughing, showing ourselves not knowing the answers, showing ourselves perfectly imperfect.

Those are some of the strongest messages that we send to our children. Our children listen to our actions, not our words.

As mums we mustn't underestimate our capacity to give other mums, to hold space for other mums to have, those moments. We do that by sharing our own moments, being in the arena with dust on our face. It's not about always listening to people who have expertise, but holding space for each other as mums to have those moments.

*In the next interview, Lucinda Button continues this explo-
ration of self-love through mindfulness.*

Key learning points

1. Learn to prioritise your own needs to be able to give
   more to other people.

2. As human beings our only real emotional need is to
   be loved.

3. Give your children space to be vulnerable and do
   not expect perfection.

4. All behaviour is a form of communication.

5. What we are praised for in our childhood, creates
   our emotional roadmap.

Additional resources

More about Brené Brown: http://brenebrown.com.

Carol Dweck's TEDx talk: www.ted.com/talks/carol_dweck_
the_power_of_believing_that_you_can_improve.

Learn self-love through mindfulness

Lucinda Button

*…know that you were doing your best in **that** moment with the awareness, understanding, experience and knowledge that you had **in that moment**.*

Lucinda Button changed career after becoming a mother. An expert in mindfulness and self-love for mums, Lucinda's journey began pre-motherhood when she was a rebellious teenager, leaving home at 17. She spent her 20s working hard and playing hard in equal measure, living a hedonistic lifestyle while holding good 'career' jobs. All along she knew she was trying to fill a void within, with hedonism, materialism and external success.

LB: I look back now and although I wasn't conscious of it, I was living in pain with low self-esteem. Not physical pain, but that nagging emotional not-feeling-great-about-myself pain. I had a feeling that it would change once I became a mother.

My first son was born after a traumatic labour which was difficult to cope with afterwards. Having a baby is a big change, even if you have a settled baby. We don't honour that in this society; there's no initiation into motherhood in our culture, unlike some other cultures around the world. It's a hard transition, especially if you've been a career woman. He had reflux from day two. He screamed and was unsettled for six months. Dealing with a baby when he's in pain all the time and there's not a lot you can do about it... it's really, really difficult.

On day two, bringing him home from hospital – my heart burst open. The feeling of unconditional love I wanted to give him, to believe in him, to be interested in his hopes and dreams. To be there for him completely. At the same time, it hit me that this wasn't what I'd experienced in my life. That was the first seed of awareness on my journey.

He became a challenging toddler, meltdowns, extreme emotional outbursts... I wasn't in a great place so I found it difficult to cope. I suffered with anxiety and depression. We had another baby, we moved house, renovated a house and it was too much. We're all human and I had a breakdown. I like to call it my breakthrough.

I like to think of personal growth as onion layers. Through our life experience, things happen and onion layers build up. Everyone has different onion layers; different thicknesses with their own unique journey through life. We can go on a purposeful journey with intention to remove these onion layers and get to our true self. Or we can go through a big emotional experience like I did when loads of these onion layers were ripped off at once.

SB: *Your initial experience of being a mother was not the easiest.*

LB: No, and I grieved. I grieved the experience I thought I was going to have. That giggly happy baby, that bonding. My baby was in pain all the time, screaming. And there was nothing I could do. I tried everything, I turned into a Google monster doctor trying to figure out what was wrong with him. It was a tough time.

SB: *I had severe postnatal depression after my first and I remember being envious of mums that seemed to be in love with their babies and with being a mother.*

LB: We're fed this message through the media of the perfect mother, the perfect life. When your experience doesn't live up to that it can be tough.

I had that complete flood of unconditional love – I know it's not like that for all mums so I feel lucky I experienced that. Love was the foundation; then awareness. I read *The Power of Now* by Eckhart Tolle. Those things together started my journey to conscious parenting.

I started noticing my onion layers. I went on a journey to peel off those layers: the ancestral heritage of how you've been parented, your family and societal conditioning and any emotional wounding you might be carrying from unmet childhood needs, life experiences and self-limiting beliefs.

I realised what I wanted was to touch as many mamas, mums and their children as possible through their own journeys of conscious parenting, with the foundation of mindfulness and self-love to become the conscious parent.

SB: *What is mindfulness?*

LB: Some people think mindfulness is something you have to do, when actually it is just paying attention to ourselves. It's so simple. It's a practice in tuning in or noticing your whole experience in the present moment.

It's a muscle that isn't developed in the Western world. We live in our minds so much. The word mindfulness brings up thoughts and ideas about it being about thinking purposefully about something. It's a lot more than that. It's coming into our bodies and our feelings, our whole experience in the now, this moment now. Rather than jumping onto one thought cloud after another. We're so far away in our mind, from our present experience in the moment, we're thinking about the past and future and we're not in the present.

It's about noticing the mind but not being carried away into our subconscious. It's about noticing and not going off into autopilot; bringing yourself back and being completely present in the moment.

There are different ways of being present in the moment. First there's the physical – tuning into your senses, your body sensations. It's a great way to start the practice of mindfulness through the body and the physical sensations.

Then there's the emotions or our feelings, without going into a story about why we're feeling that way. It's noticing those emotions; noticing that they're there. Letting yourself feel the emotion without reacting based on that emotion. Noticing and not reacting.

The tricky one is the exterior: what is out of ourselves when we communicate with others, what's in the environment beyond ourselves.

Building a muscle of mindfulness requires practice. Start by catching moments of awareness through the day, for example if you're washing up or stuck at the traffic lights, you might have a moment of consciousness.

Anchor yourself in the present moment – if you're driving the car, for example, feel the sensation of your hands on the steering wheel. Maybe feel your thighs and your back against the chair, feel your feet on the floor and use your physical sensations to ground yourself in the moment. Notice your breathing. We all breathe all the time, but we don't notice that we're doing it. It's a good way to tune into the present moment by noticing and following your breathing.

It's a direction of attention. It's so simple and it's a practice to build up. Catch moments during the day and ground yourself in the present moment. Or go deeper into a five-minute meditation.

SB: *What is the benefit of mindfulness?*

LB: We can choose our reactions in the present moment. For example if our children are not doing what we want them to do, triggering our need to control. We might react and shout which we wouldn't choose to do *if* we were reacting from a place of consciousness.

The more we're able to build this muscle of mindfulness, the more we're able to stay present with ourselves so we can react from a place where we want to react from; our true selves rather than what's being brought up by strong emotions or things in our external environment.

The journey of conscious parenting is knowing that we're not perfect. We're doing our best. If we do shout and you look back and think, 'I wish I didn't do that, that wasn't how I wanted to react,' know that you were doing your best in **that** moment with the awareness, understanding, experience and knowledge that you had. If you knew differently you would have done differently. It's to treat ourselves as we were at that time, with compassion, and to be better next time.

It's a journey. Our children bring up stuff for us from our childhood. We say things that our parents maybe said. Our children help us to see our areas for growth, what isn't serving us; and what controls us.

SB: *Choosing how to react can engender calmness which becomes self-perpetuating.*

LB: I would like to share something practical: the four Ds. If you catch a moment when you're feeling strong emotions:

- First, **Deep breathing** – take one, two or three deep breaths.

- Second is to **Drop**. Drop into your body, feel into your body, feel the softening, and ground yourself. Feel your feet touching the floor, feel your legs so that it creates a feeling of grounding into the present moment.

- That gives you space to **Decide**. You can choose your reaction with awareness rather than unconsciously reacting from your 'stuff' or your onion layers.

- Finally **Delve**. That might be at the time or maybe that evening you can delve into what happened. Be curious as to why you reacted in that way; what was underneath and what's underneath that. It's about a journey of awareness.

SB: *Toni Brodelle talked about behaviour being a form of communication. You're talking about your behaviour as communication to yourself about what you need to explore.*

LB: Yes and it's important to always be kind to ourselves. Take on board and understand that every person is doing their best in the moment with what they have at the time. It's about treating ourselves with the same love and compassion that we treat our children.

SB: *You've been practising mindfulness for some time, what differences do you notice?*

LB: I've cleared away so much of my own stuff. We can't change anything in our lives if we're not aware of it first. Awareness is the key to any growth or change and mindfulness brings that awareness.

My relationship with my children is much better. It's helped my confidence. Being connected with my true self and what I'm here to do, that I'm good enough. It's freed me of the negative chatter we might have in our heads.

I find in my work with clients that there are foundation limiting beliefs such as 'I'm not good enough' or 'don't shine your light too brightly'. What sits on top are more specific personal limiting beliefs: 'I'm too ugly, too fat, too stupid.'

Practising mindfulness starts bringing awareness to how we're thinking. We start noticing how we're thinking and how we talk to ourselves; we can change that. A limiting belief is a thought that we have had for so long that it's taken root and turned into a belief. The beauty with thoughts is that we can change them.

There is an amazing poem, *The Guest House,* by Jelaluddin Rumi. He describes us as a guest house and every new visitor that comes to the door is a different emotion, a different feeling. We open the door to each one with the same response, welcome. It's only if we bury feelings and hold them down that they fester and pop up at inopportune moments, maybe in our parenting.

It is part of self-love: treating ourselves kindly and with compassion. The food we eat, the exercise we do – it all starts from the thoughts we have about our body. If we love our body, and we feel good about ourselves, thinking we are good enough, then naturally we start making choices that look after our body. There's no other us so if we can live our life as our best friend, it's a whole lot sweeter.

Self-love is being kind and compassionate to ourselves. It's difficult to be kind and compassionate to others if we're not kind and compassionate to ourselves first.

We can't know anything or do anything until we have awareness. One of the ways to get awareness is through practising mindfulness. If we had needs as children that weren't met, that can create emotional wounding. We carry through ancestral heritage of how we were parented. Historically a lot of people have been parented in that top-down, very punishment/discipline way: 'I am greater than you because I'm your parent.'

I recommend Dr Shefali Tsabary and her book *The Conscious Parent*.

Conscious parenting is about modelling; about becoming the safe vessel to hold our children in their growth. For example when they're showing their big scary strong emotions, we're able to be there with them, with their emotions and not react from them.

Modelling is important, not to hide our feelings but to honour them. If I'm feeling really angry, 'I'm feeling really angry right now,' instead of 'Oh you make me so angry, because of what you did.' Owning the emotion. Emotion is not bad. Anger is helpful because it can bring up deep stuff and show that we feel something is unjust. It's a healthy emotion. It becomes unhealthy when we don't own it and we dump it on others rather than dealing with that painful emotion. If we hide our emotions, and don't acknowledge them, our children will copy and do the same thing.

Often those scary big feelings that children have, we don't want to see them. We say, 'You'll be fine.' It teaches children to internalise and hide those feelings; that it's not ok to feel them. Modelling is very important.

Mindfulness gives you the growth of awareness. Self-love raises our self-esteem and there's the knock-on effect of our children's self-esteem rising. When we're able to recognise our needs and prioritise our needs, we make positive choices.

Sometimes before we can show ourselves self-love, we need to clear away our past and this is what the next interview with Maxine Harley explores.

Key learning points

1. The journey of conscious parenting is knowing that we're not perfect.

2. Self-love is being kind and compassionate to ourselves.

3. Practising mindfulness allows us to choose our reactions in the present moment.

4. Choosing how to react can engender calmness, which becomes self-perpetuating.

Additional resources

Conscious Parenting, Shefali Tsabary at TEDxSF: www. youtube.com/watch?v=QM_PQ2WUD2k.

Clear away your past – no matter how you were parented

I lashed out at my daughter... The look of fear on her face and in her eyes shocked me. It hit me in the heart because I knew that feeling too many times as a child. We all have unhealed emotional wounds and they bleed a little each day.

Maxine Harley has 20 years' experience as a counsellor and psychotherapist. She is a Mind Healer and Personal Development Consultant, and published writer. Her passion is to help mums be the best mums they can be by reparenting themselves and clearing away the emotional blocks that may get in the way. Maxine herself experienced a tough childhood.

MH: I was emotionally and physically abused and neglected. Not so badly that I completely unravelled. I now know that this pattern can be changed and turned around for the next generation to create a more positive ripple effect.

I grew up feeling empty inside, wearing masks and playing games to get my needs met. I had several troubled adult relationships with unavailable men like my father, or insecure and needy men who were like my mother. I had a confident mask which was hiding the real me underneath. I didn't even know who the real me was.

After months of struggling alone as a single parent on benefits, my defences were low and I lashed out at my little daughter for doing something minor. The look of fear on her face and in her eyes shocked me. It hit me in the heart because I knew that feeling too many times as a child. First things first, I repaired the tear in our relationship. I vowed then to sort myself out, whatever that took and not to allow history to repeat itself. We all have unhealed emotional wounds and they bleed a little each day. When we are over-whelmed and our defences are low, struggling to cope, these wounds can burst open and badly affect the people around us too.

Since that time, I have trained and qualified as a counsellor and psychotherapist. I now work with mums and mums-to-be.

There's a real need to raise our own self-esteem to be able to consistently help our children to do that. The relationship you have with yourself affects every-body around you so it's of primary importance. Con-fidence can be elusive. You might have confidence in other roles, such as in the workplace, but not as a parent. Being a mum is a big responsibility. There's often a fear of being judged and getting it wrong, not really trusting your own intuition and opinions. We know that postnatal depression can be a response to childhood wounds being opened up. There's more interest and focus on the past and how that affects the now and the future too.

There are two aspects to us. The persona that we want people to see – we try to convince them that this is the real us; then there is the real you behind, struggling to cope. In recent years we have learned more about how our brains are shaped and how they change in the early years.

Later things influence us too, but those first three years are extremely important. There are aspects of neuroscience such as the effects of oxytocin (that cuddling and bonding hormone) that we didn't know years ago.

Trauma and emotional wounds affect the emotional part of our brain, particularly an area called the amygdala, in the middle of your brain. The amygdala is involved in bonding with others. When that is impacted by our experiences, it affects our ability to be able to connect and bond with other people.

There are several things that can get in the way of a child having a happy childhood. Obvious things like chronic illness, extended hospitalisation and surgery, poverty, deprivation, emotional trauma such as a losing parent, but perhaps the most significant factor is the emotional state of the parents, especially the mother.

There are some appalling parents out there at the extreme end of the spectrum with addictions, chaos, intentional violence, sexual and physical abuse and neglect. That often results in personality disorders and even death of the child in some cases.

Then we have the 'nowhere near good enough parents'. These are the parents that probably don't get picked up by the authorities and the child suffers in silence. The parents play mind games, they confuse the child, they're cold and cruel, use harsh discipline and punishments without explanation, they exert control and authority without flexibility. Abuse exists but it's hidden and the children are forbidden from telling anyone which leaves the child feeling isolated and helpless. They learn to hide away within themselves and not to expect love or care. There are many people with this experience, often hidden behind the mask.

We have 'not good enough' parenting where the child doesn't feel loved for who they are. They may have had well-meaning parents who bought them lots of toys, they went to good schools, wore lovely clothes, but the parents didn't spend time with the children. Maybe due to work or ill-health, perhaps grieving over the loss of other family members. We're not blaming anybody for this. People do the best with what they've got.

The important 'good enough' parenting is about doing the best you can with what you know and what you have. Feeling good enough as a person to be a good enough mum. Yes, you make the odd mistake but you put it right as soon as possible. In an ideal world we give the child a sense of emotional bonding, we're attuned to the child's needs before they're expressed. We're mirroring the young child with matching facial expressions and verbal sounds. We're creating a secure, unconditional, emotional attachment. It's assisting your child to develop a positive and robust self-esteem of their own, a sense of their own power and their own competency; we encourage them to have good relationship skills, we're modelling good self-regulation.

Good enough parenting encourages emotional intelligence so children can name, understand and manage their emotions and form good emotional connections with other people. Emotional intelligence is a greater predictor of happiness and success than IQ.

Finally we have 'optimum parenting' which has all the facets of good enough parenting and a bit more. By intentionally facing and clearing away our personal obstacles to achieving good enough parenting, we optimise our emotional availability for the child. We become consciously aware. A part of us that can reflect on what we are doing, learn from it and grow; being able to know and trust yourself and your own instincts and your own opinions; creating the best environment to nurture a balanced and happy child.

It's about avoiding the three big mistakes that we make:

- not healing our own emotional wounds,

- not taking care of our own deeper emotional needs; perhaps you might be resentful of the needs of a small child because the child in you is saying 'What about me?'

- not controlling ourselves – by that I mean our thought processes, our emotions, our speech and our behaviour.

People don't do this on purpose; these are not intentional mistakes. People just don't know how not to make them or how not to pass on their past to the future of their children.

My approach to dealing with this is to focus on the whole person. I advocate that parents should reparent themselves and heal their own emotional wounds to enable them to become better parents to the next generation. Care and repair from the inside out.

The positive takeaway is you can change anything you want to change when you become aware of it and you have the right knowledge and skills to put into practice.

Some of us have an inkling of our emotional wounds. We sound like our parents or we have over-reacted to something. Not because we're tired but we have this hidden in the shadows feeling, that history is repeating itself. Ask yourself, 'What if this is mine? What bit have I got to own up to and look at?' We've all got stuff.

People can feel lonely and isolated when a new baby arrives, particularly if there are issues in the relationship that having a new baby might have influenced and sometimes made worse. There is that profound sense of loneliness and not knowing who to reach out to and how to heal that wound.

SB: *In my work with parents, many mums tell me their relationship with their own mother changes when they become a mother. More intense and closer.*

MH: It can work both ways. Sometimes relationships with your mother become fraught. As a mum, you want the very best for your child. You might think, 'Hang on a minute. Why didn't I get this?' It can enhance that bond, particularly when the grandma becomes involved and creates a new relationship with their child and their grandchildren.

SB: *What else can we do to be the best parent and clear away some of that stuff from our own childhood?*

MH: It's a process and it starts with self-awareness. If you have a habit of giving yourself a hard time, ask yourself, 'Would I do this to my child? Would I treat my child like this?' We all have an inner child inside and this is the part of us that was wounded. The greatest healing is when we can access that part. Keep checking in: how am I doing? What do I need? What is going on for me right now? Not in a narcissistic, self-absorbed way but you need to take your own self-esteem as high as you can, by focusing on the things that you get right and the things that you can do right.

SB: *As a new parent, it is important to give ourselves permission to be a beginner. We're learning what works and what's best for ourselves and our children.*

MH: We get so much contradictory advice as well. Slow down, calm down and think, what went right today? If there's anything that didn't go well, what do you need to do about it? Do this calmly without being overly emotional.

SB: *Being a good enough mother some of the time is enough.*

MH: Exactly. If there is a tear in the relationship, because something happens, as soon as possible, soothe the child, talk in that soft loving voice, calm everything down, lift the mood and get back onto that nice emotional level. It's difficult to know the effect that we have on our children because the first two or three years are pre-verbal. The child remembers things subconsciously. They might have a bodily or somatic memory of events but they won't have a verbal narrative. Their brain isn't developed enough to have that.

The first two or three years of life are pre-verbal – the child can't tell you what's wrong and what she needs but she's soaking up everything. Up to the age of about six, children are like sponges that absorb everything. They are forming their own subconscious belief system; I call it a script. That script will run their lives about 95% of the time for the rest of their lives. Those early years are really important.

What is fascinating about neuroscience is that the brain can change itself: neuroplasticity. Based on new experiences, it can rewire itself, it can grow new connections and one part can compensate for another part that is not working so well; one part can grow larger if needed. It's never too late to change things.

MH: We can't generalise but we know enough to know that we can rewire our brains. To change our behaviour on average takes 66 days. It takes about 21 days to change the way you see yourself, but to change your **behaviour** takes 66 days. That's an average.

Don't give yourself a hard time because you're not changing your behaviour straight away. It takes time for the new behaviour to become automatic and be easier than the old behaviour. When you put new practices into place, stick with it and remind yourself that on average it's going to take 66 days.

With persistence and repetition we can rewire the brain and learn new behaviours. There's always hope.

SB: *There have been so many neuroscience discoveries and we don't know yet what research is going to come along. I'm thinking I need a change of career to study neuroscience.*

MH: If I had my life again I'd become a neuroscientist.

We have explored how showing self-love, building our self-esteem, mindfulness, and clearing away our past help to build our emotional wellbeing. In the next interview with Elaine Halligan and Melissa Hood of The Parent Practice, we explore how to raise the self-esteem of our children.

Key learning points

1. There are two aspects to all of us: the persona you want people to see and the real you behind.

2. 'Good enough' parenting encourages emotional intelligence, which is a predictor of happiness and success.

3. Parents need to heal their own emotional wounds to be better parents to the next generation.

4. Healing your emotional wounds starts with self-awareness.

5. It takes on average 66 days to change your behaviour.

How parents can raise the self-esteem of their children

Elaine Halligan and Melissa Hood

Descriptive praise works better than evaluative praise because it takes more effort on the parent's part.

Elaine Halligan and Melissa Hood are the directors of The Parent Practice, which is at the forefront of the parenting world, real parenting for real kids. Their practice draws on the latest thinking in psychology, neuroscience and psychotherapy. They work with parents and carers, schools and nurseries, corporate and business clients. Their aim is to pass on their parenting skills to help parents bring up children to be happy and the best they can be. Founding director Melissa, head of training, programme design & development, heads up the Australian office while Elaine heads up the London office. Both have experienced their own parenting challenges.

EH: The impact we have on our children's behaviour is phenomenal; what we do and what we say in the moment has the biggest impact on what happens next. Feeling more cooperative and motivated to get things right is at the heart of everything we do at The Parent Practice, how to be positive but firm and how to be consistent.

When a child's self-esteem is low, you will often see this in poor behaviour. If a child has good self-esteem, if their sense of self is strong, they're willing to try things. If they don't believe in themselves, why bother trying? If they don't believe they can succeed, there's not much point in putting in the effort. And they give up, whether we're talking in an academic context or otherwise.

Self-esteem is at the core of self-belief and self-worth. One of the ways you can raise self-esteem is how you talk to your children.

EH: Descriptive praise is key. Some people talk to their children and they are positive saying things like 'good boy', 'good girl', 'well done', 'you're a superstar', 'you're amazing'… That praise is good but it doesn't give the child any information about what they've done well in order to replicate it. If you tell a child over and over again that they are amazing or you tell them they're a superstar when they came third in the race, but they wanted to come first, they won't believe you.

Most people praise their children evaluatively – an evaluation of what they believe they've done. Evaluative praise is positive and it's better than being negative. We need to start praising more effectively by praising descriptively. With descriptive praise you give an illustration of *why* the picture was good, for example. Have they thought hard about the colours to use, have they planned ahead to get the composition right? Have they rubbed something out to self-correct?

MH: Descriptive praise works better than evaluative praise because it takes more effort on the parent's part. Your children know that you have taken more effort and were paying attention. It's more meaningful and sincere so our children get more out of it.

Paying attention to our children is one of the key things that we do as a parent. Our children are hard-wired to want our attention. If we pay attention to what they're doing wrong and talk about that, they're getting attention negatively. We need to turn that around with our children and pay more attention to the positive things that they're doing.

MH: One of the downsides of evaluative praise is that sometimes it's comparative. We want children to feel good about themselves for themselves without being competitive.

EH: If there's sibling rivalry sometimes inadvertently we promote it by saying things like, 'Who can get up the stairs quickest for the bath?' 'Who can finish their meal first?' For a child with a competitive spirit that can make them even more competitive.

MH: We want children to feel that they're the best they can be, not compared to anyone else but for themselves. To have a realistic assessment of who they are and appreciate them for who they are.

If you're being descriptive you will, by definition, be congruent. You'll be sincere and be credible because you're describing what your child is doing that you value.

EH: It is important to acknowledge children not just on the end result but on the journey or the process. We encourage parents to acknowledge the effort children make; the improvement they're making, the progress, the strategies they're using in addition to the end result. Focus on change and you will get better results.

MH: In the research by Professor Carol Dweck, she talks about a difference between the growth mindset and the fixed mindset. In the growth mindset a child is really interested in growing and open to ways of changing. The child knows that by their own efforts they can make improvements. A child with a fixed mindset thinks that they've got a finite amount of intelligence and if they fail at something, it means they're not smart enough and there's nothing they can do about it. That child is very worried about protecting their status as an intelligent person; whereas a growth-mindset child is willing to deal with failure because they know that they simply need to try a different strategy or try harder or work longer.

We want our children to have a growth mindset. Dweck's research shows very clearly that the way parents talk to children about their efforts makes a difference to what mindset they develop. If your child takes part in sport, and the parent says, 'Did you win?' as the first question, they get a strong idea that winning is important. Whereas if your questions are about how the game went – 'Did everybody play well together? Were you passing the ball between team members? Did you manage to set up a goal for someone else? Were you listening to the coach?' – those questions put more emphasis on strategies and effort than on the outcome of the game.

EH: It is about context. We don't believe that everyone's a winner. Winning is at times important but it's not the only thing. The idea is that your children won't win all the time. The way we build up their self-esteem is by focusing on other things, such as 'Did you listen to the coach?'

MH: We need to teach our children how to cope with failure; one way they can cope is by having a sturdy self-esteem that understands that, 'OK I didn't win this time but I did my best and if I keep working on it I will win next time.'

MH: Praise should be focused on strategies, effort and small improvements, and also attitude.

EH: Parents might say, 'Oh you're very clever' or 'you're very bright'. Carol Dweck took two groups of children and gave them puzzles to solve. Both groups were able to do this puzzle quickly and easily. The first group of children were praised for the effort, the attitude, and persevering. The second group of children were told, 'Wow, you must be really clever.'

Each group of children was presented with an even harder puzzle. The second group of children, praised for being really clever, gave up when presented with something that was much harder. They wanted to go back to the easier puzzle.

EH: The children praised for effort, attitude, and progress chose to do the harder one and gave it a go, illustrating that they had a growth mindset. They didn't mind if they got it wrong; it was about giving it a go.

EH: We do need to set up opportunities for our children to succeed. If they have lots of experiences of failure that's not great for their self-esteem.

MH: We recommend to parents that when children have completed their homework, they find several things to descriptively praise about it but at least one thing to improve. The child gets used to the idea that making improvement doesn't mean that you're a failure.

Some children will be more sensitive than others: some will take on board feedback and they'll have no problem with it; others take it very personally. Partly that goes back to self-esteem. When our self-esteem is robust, we can accept feedback as useful. That is true for us as adults too. When you're feeling strong, you embrace feedback. If you're feeling low, feedback feels like criticism. It's hard to hear and may make you want to give up. This is one of the reasons it's so important for parents to build their children's self-esteem.

EH: There's a difference between self-esteem and confidence. My son Sam was thrown out of three schools by the age of seven. He was out of school for two years and literacy has always been a problem. Even now, aged 19, his confidence in his literacy is low. But he recognises his strengths in other areas and acknowledges his weaknesses. His sense of self-worth is high. You can have a high sense of self-esteem and be unconfident in certain areas. Strong self-esteem gives you robustness and resilience. Lack of confidence could be simply self-awareness of your strengths.

MH: What we model is important. 80% of parenting is modelling. If a child complains they're not good at maths, don't say to them, 'Well, it's because you've got my genes.'

There's a related area, which is how do children experience struggle? If the child has a growth mindset, they will embrace struggle. A fixed mindset person faced with a maths problem that they're struggling with will say, 'That means I'm no good at maths.' A growth mindset person will say, 'I need to find a different strategy or I need to practise more.' You want your children to embrace struggle so that they think it's good. Your brain grows when you struggle with something.

EH: We need to set things up so that our children have a chance to feel competent. Competence breeds confidence. We need to let them struggle with things, we need to give them tasks that are age appropriate and we need to not do too much for them. Otherwise they will not have the opportunity to demonstrate competence for themselves.

MH: As well as descriptive praise, we can raise self-esteem by giving children household tasks or chores.

It can be the tiniest things: emptying the wastepaper basket, feeding the dog, setting the table. We make them feel more competent. They feel successful and when they feel successful they get our attention in the form of praise.

A great way of capturing descriptive praise is to use the Golden Book, one for each child. Get a notebook. It doesn't need to be expensive, a simple notebook which they can decorate. You call this the Golden Book, the Praise Book – come up with a name with your children. Set yourself a target of writing at least three descriptive praises in this Golden Book for each child every day.

If it feels difficult to think of three things, ask your child to help. You want them to get into the habit of recognising their own goodness. It's not bad to ask, 'What are three things that you've done today that you can be proud of?'

EH: You can incorporate the Golden Book into the bed-time routine. It's a lovely way to finish the day.

It can be transformational. One client called me just before Christmas to say their child was out of control. Everything was going wrong, they were spending 80% of their time dealing with temper tantrums. In the first session I asked whether they had a problem with noticing the good behaviour. What was happening was this family was focusing on all the things they did not like. Our reticular activating system looks for evidence to support our belief. If you believe your child is oppositional, defiant, noncompliant, uncooperative, aggressive and always attacking his sister, the reticular activating system will focus you to look for evidence to support that theory.

MH: These parents started to notice the good things that previously had gone unnoticed. The boy's self-esteem rocketed and they saw transformational results. He needed mum and dad to notice all the good things he was doing.

Even if your children are not yet of reading age, in our culture when we write something down, we give it an extra credibility. They can look through the pages and see all the things that mum and dad appreciate; that's very good for self-esteem.

EH: When I first heard about descriptive praise I thought, great concept but you haven't met my son. When I first started, I found it difficult to descriptively praise him. I wasn't in the habit and I wasn't used to looking for the small things. I was waiting for something big to praise. It has a more motivating effect if we look for the small things. If this is the first time you've heard of descriptive praise, give yourself permission to be a beginner.

Descriptive praise, how are you going to do it? You are going to do it verbally. When the children are doing the right thing and you want to acknowledge them for it, instead of setting up a complicated star chart, let's get really simple and set up the pasta jar.

Children love visual representations of how successful they are being. Whenever the children do something right or put a smile on your face or show a helping hand, you can acknowledge them physically and visibly by putting a piece of dried pasta in a jar. It's a way of letting them know how successful they've been. Be generous with it. Make the pasta jar small. Small jar, big pasta. One jar for all the children – don't set it up so they are in competition.

EH: Once the pasta is in, it stays in. Please don't remove the pasta. Can you imagine how demotivating it is to take pasta out? If your child asks for a piece themselves to put in, that means that they're really aware of their behaviour and what they can do to earn acknowledgement when they do the right thing.

When the pasta jar is full (it needs to fill up quickly, within two or three days), give your children an extra special reward. We encourage parents to use non-material rewards, for example, spending time with the parent playing a game or reading a book.

EH: If you are starting descriptive praise as a new skill, for the first time, then do let your children know what you are doing. Tell them you are learning to be a parent through The Confident Mother and you realise that in the past you may have focused too much on the negatives. Be patient, explain to your child 'I'm trying to focus on all the good things that you're doing.' Give some examples of things that you can praise the child for.

MH: Do be careful not to patronise your children, don't praise them for things that are well within their abilities. If you praised a 16 year old for tying his own shoelaces, he's going to think that you've sprouted another head. Make sure it's relevant praise.

Key learning points

1. Use descriptive praise.

2. Set your child up to succeed but don't let them be afraid of failure.

3. Encourage growth mindset by praising progress, effort and persistence, and not just achievement.

4. Use the Golden Book to record progress.

5. Small jar, big pasta.

Additional resources

'Don't call your child clever' blog post: www.theparentpractice.com/blog/dont-call-your-child-clever.

The Parent Practice publish their book *Real Parenting for Real Kids* in April 2016.

The working mums and business mums that I work with often worry about how little quality time they spend with their children. In the next interview, Richard Curtis shares strategies and ideas on how to make the most of the time you do have.

Make the most of the time you have with your children

Richard Curtis

Richard Curtis, The Kid Calmer, was a teacher in his former life. His background is in working with children with extreme behavioural difficulties. He moved away from the classroom six or seven years ago to work with schools, helping head teachers and now spends much of his time helping families. Richard is up front that he doesn't have children himself; however the techniques that he shares, he has used with families and with teachers working with children. At The Confident Mother conference, Richard agreed to share his ideas for making the most of the time that we do have with our children.

Adults are not always right.

RC: I firmly believe that it is very important that you have family rules: what the expectation is for behaviour, what the sanctions or the consequence are. I prefer to use the word consequence. It is important that we are teaching our children how to do their best. In my 30 Day Parenting Challenge, the first few days are about setting up the systems in your family. Then we go on to trying different things, different techniques over the next 20 days or so to change the nature of the time you have with your children

For example – it's rare that we let children talk uninterrupted. Think about conversations that you have with your children and with your family, often you finish each other's sentences or jump in before someone has finished talking. At meal times, take it in turns to speak uninterrupted for two, three, five minutes.

We want to fill the silence. Let the silence grow. If it's Johnny's turn to talk, if he sits there in silence for 15 seconds, just let that silence 'be'. Don't interrupt his silence. Allowing the time (and the silence) is important for the development of self-esteem and development of identity. It's a technique used for children with speech and language difficulties as well. A compounding issue can be the stress of someone trying to guess what you're saying.

You start finding out things about your children and what they think. You would not have found that out if you hadn't let them talk uninterrupted.

RC: Another exercise which has huge impact when spending time with your child is to **let them lead the play**. This is based on the principle that as adults we are self-inhibiting. We stop ourselves doing so many things; we put in our own boundaries. Children don't have those boundaries or limiting beliefs. It's good for your child to see you letting yourself go. Let the child tell you who you've got to be and what to do.

For example, if you ask your child, 'Where are you going to go in a cardboard box today?' They might say, 'I'm going to Mars in a car.' If we lead that play

as adults, we would insist that the cardboard box is a rocket, because contextually that's our limiting belief. It's good fun to let yourself go, be present at your child's level and let them direct your play.

RC: Don't kick yourself about the amount of time you have with your children. The more time you spend feeling guilty about the lack of time that you have with your children, the less time you are engaged with your children. We all do the best that we can. There are only 24 hours in the day and you can't magic up more time. As working parents, it's part of the lifestyle that we choose and so it's important to change the nature of that time.

RC: Optimise the limited time you have with your children. You can't increase it but optimise it as best you can. Be fully present at those times. Phone, work, email – turn it off when you're with your family. There has to be a work/life balance. If you're with your family, focus on that and turn the emails or phone off. You can catch up later. Let's be honest, if you hear your phone buzzing, your mind wanders.

RC: Switch yourself off from work, and that will help to clear different parts of the brain so that when you return, it frees up your mind to be processing things without consciously thinking of it. The principle is that sometimes we need to empty out the temporal lobes in our brain.

RC: There's a lot of evidence to support the fact that this happens to children who spend a lot of time on game machines and electronic devices immediately before bed or who watch stimulating DVDs before bed. It fills the front part of the brain with thoughts and reactions, and different emotions. When the child goes to bed, they need time to clear that out before they go to sleep, so build in time in the routine to let that happen.

RC: We know about the power of reading a story with our children. If you're snuggled up with your child and reading a book with them or to them, effectively you are mirroring what you did when they were a baby. When you are a baby, in the first few weeks, as adults we hug you, we get close to you, we share body warmth, maybe we rock you and we speak softly and calmly. We use our voice in a regular pattern to help soothe and to calm the baby. When you read a book with your child, this replicates a similar emotion within the child.

RC: It's about accessing the core of our inner self. There are many ways of accessing your core inner self when you're overwhelmed or experiencing difficulties. For a child to sleep, it helps if you can get them to that point before bed.

RC: When a child is older and grown out of bedtime stories, it might be having a bath or a shower. It might be reading a book themselves.

SB: *Accessing that core inner self before you go to bed, not looking at electronic gadgets or screens, calms* down your brain so that you can go to sleep more easily.

Adults are not always right...

RC: Anyone who knows me will have heard me say this very passionately: adults are not always right.

If we spend our limited time with our children being a dictator, the risk is that our children grow up to be dictators or grow up expecting to be dictated to.

If you can teach your children what to do when you get things wrong and how to deal with it, you are teaching your children a life skill: negotiating and problem-solving. Today's society is not 'children are seen but not heard'. In fact, we need to bring up our children to deal with *tomorrow's* world, not today's.

Be open about your emotions: if you're cross, or proud. If we can help children recognise their emotions it could potentially have a generational effect. Teenagers who attempt suicide, for example, predominantly that is related to an overwhelming emotion. They are experiencing an emotion and struggling to cope with it. If we can teach our children how to cope with those emotions, to cope with being overwhelmed, that will have an effect in the future.

Talking about the naughty step

RC: I am adamant that the naughty step should be banned. Your child is five, they've done something wrong so they have to sit on the naughty step for five minutes and think about what they've done. If they get up, you put them back down. Eventually you're in a situation where you're *holding* them on the naughty step, which is traumatic enough, but a child doesn't learn. We don't have the internal monologue, the ability to reflect on things until we are seven or eight. How can a five year old spend five minutes thinking about what they've done? They'll think about something else or they'll withdraw. It doesn't work so get rid of the naughty step.

Instead, I'm a great advocate of the child's voice. Even two or three year olds can tell you what is right and wrong at a simplistic level. Sit down as a family and agree what the family rules are and the sanctions. For some children, saying sorry is enough. That's important. By helping children to say 'sorry' and to learn those manners from an early age we're teaching them the rules of society.

RC: It's been proven that smacking doesn't work; it's traumatic, it has long-term implications, and children repeat offend within 10 minutes after being smacked.

SB: *If you feel tempted to smack, what do you suggest we do to stop ourselves?*

RC: I would challenge parents – that moment in time is not the right time to use a sanction. They are trying to satisfy their own needs at that point. They need to walk away or stand back. It's about how we feel as the adult in that moment; it's about our containment and deciding, 'No, I'm going to hold myself. I'll deal with this in a few minutes and come back to it.'

SB: *What are your final tips on being present and making sure that time with our children is quality time?*

RC: Focus on being present and not feeling guilty. If you have the system in place as a family, if you have the rules and the consequences in place, that gives you a quick win because you don't have to spend your time thinking up new rules and sanctions. You have a system in place to do that for you; instead use the time to enjoy being with your children. It makes a huge difference.

Key learning points

1. Let your children lead the play.

2. Focus on being fully present when you are with your children.

3. Don't waste the time you have feeling guilty.

4. Set family rules and consequences.

5. Be open about your emotions.

6. If you feel tempted to smack, walk away.

My own session was aimed at helping mums to ditch the guilt.

Ditch the guilt

Sherry Bevan

Often it can be hard to balance being a mum with work. Sherry Bevan is The Confidence Guide, and knows all about this.

After more than 25 years working in professional services, coming back from an almost fatal head injury on the race circuit, two bouts of severe postnatal depression, retraining as a breastfeeding counsellor, and later as a confidence coach, Sherry set up her business in 2012 to have more quality time with her children.

Sherry uses her inner strength and confidence to nurture and inspire mums to make life-changing decisions with ease. Sherry is an action taker and she knows exactly how to help you overcome the confidence blocks and inertia that are keeping you stuck.

What she notices, though, is that so many working mums, regardless of whether they work for an employer or run their own businesses, are in constant danger of being overwhelmed by guilt, especially during the school holidays.

We hear about the working mum and I wondered, what about the working dad? I did a Google search on 'working mum guilt': 534,000 results came back. Yet amazingly, when I searched 'working dad guilt', there were 17,500,000 results. I was shocked. Why is there such a HUGE difference? I was honestly expecting the difference to be the other way round. Surely there are not more commentators and articles on working dads than there are on working mums? Even if I change the spelling to the more US-centric 'working mom guilt', I only get 1,980,000 results.

What is going on? Is this equality for the sexes gone completely wrong? Working mums don't even get the lion's share of guilt?

There was research published by the Pew Research Center in the April 2015 issue of *Journal of Marriage and Family* which essentially tells us that working dads feel as much guilt as working mums. Almost half of working dads feel that they do not have enough time with their children.

Quite honestly I'm conflicted here. It's fantastic that dads (and therefore society) have woken up to the fact that children need them. Dads feel the conflict of working long hours and the increased expectations of them as parents. Yet why is it in newspapers, on blog posts, in job interviews – so often I hear from working mum clients, that she was asked about her childcare arrangements and the working dad is not? Why are there SO many more results on 'working dad guilt' or 'how to be a happy working dad' than for working mums?

Search Results (Google, 7 April 2015)

- Working mum guilt – 534,000

- Working mom guilt – 1,980,000

- Working dad guilt – 17,500,000

- How to be happy working mum – 13,600,000

- How to be happy working dad – 50,300,000

Are you a working mum or business mum dealing with guilt?

Do you struggle to balance work and family life? Do you worry you are damaging your relationship with your children? What follows is a modified version of my *Working Mum's Guide to Ditching the Guilt* available to purchase at my website as six downloadable audio modules with accompanying workbooks (see 'Additional resources' below).

Before you work through this section, I encourage you to find time and a quiet space, with pen and paper to hand.

The six steps to ditch the working mum's guilt.

1. BEING A MUM – what is most important to you

2. UNDERSTANDING – what is guilt, and understand your own personal guilt triggers

3. SELF-APPRECIATION – your current situation, your strengths, your experiences and your skills

4. BRAINSTORMING – the actions or steps you can take, explore alternatives and options

5. ACTION – create your action plan and put strategies in place

6. REINFORCEMENT – turn small changes into positive habits

Step 1 – being a mum

What is really important to you about being a mum? What really matters to you? Let's assume for the moment that you ARE the best mum in the world, what are you doing?

What are you saying? What are you thinking? What are you feeling? What are others saying?

And what about your children, what are they saying or feeling or thinking?

Go back in time to your childhood. What are your most cherished childhood memories of your mum? What do you most remember about your own mum? What was the most important thing to you about what your mum did or said?

Take yourself forward in time – you are now an old lady in her 80s, sitting in her rocking chair, on the porch, looking back through her photograph albums, remembering when her children were little. What do you want to remember about being a mum? What are you doing in the photographs? What are you thinking, saying, feeling? What are other people saying about you as a mum? What are your children saying about you as a mum?

Bring yourself back to the present time and answer this one question: **What is most important to you about being a mum?**

Step 2 – understanding

This quote says it all to me:

> *Guilt is not a response to anger; it is a response*
> *to one's own actions or lack of action. If it leads*
> *to change then it can be useful, since it is then*
> *no longer guilt but the beginning of knowledge.*
> Audre Lorde, *Sister Outsider: Essays and Speeches.*

Another quote from Ann Diehl about working mums:

I think we're seeing in working mothers a change from 'Thank God it's Friday' to 'Thank God it's Monday.' If any working mother has not experienced that feeling, her children are not adolescent.

I know I recognise that feeling.

The point is this. Guilt exists to tell us that we are hurting someone or doing something wrong. At least it is our PERCEPTION that we are hurting someone or doing something that we believe to be wrong. But feeling guilty does not MAKE you guilty. It does not mean that what you are doing or thinking or feeling is wrong. It could be a sign, 'I need to let go.' It could be a sign that you are falling into a mind trap. It could be a sign that there is something in your life that needs addressing.

Are you a perfectionist who doesn't like to compromise; who wants everything to be just right, who wants to do everything herself? Are you the superhero mum who tries to take on absolutely everything – from running the team at work to hand-sewing all the costumes for the school play?

Perhaps you have unrealistic expectations about what you can achieve in the hours available?

Jane Adams, research psychologist, suggests that 'Guilt is an internal state that is self-defeating and self-absorbing… Guilt is all about you, not the subject of your feelings.'

Guilt is a complex emotion. What is important is that you acknowledge and investigate the guilt that you feel. Then you can decide whether or not that guilt is justified and whether you want to do something about it.

What are your triggers? Notice these. Become aware. Where are you and who are you with?

Step 3 – self-appreciation

It is important to appreciate yourself and what you do as a mother. To take stock of your current situation, your strengths, your experiences and your skills. These are different for every woman, for every mother, for every parent.

Ask yourself:

- What do you do already? What is special about you as a mum? What do you do for your children that nobody else does?

- What else do you do? What are your limitations? What are your boundaries? What stops you doing more or less or different?

- What are your strengths? What are your special skills?

Step 4 – brainstorming

The next stage is to brainstorm all the possible options.

Here are some trigger questions to ask yourself:

- What could you do to be the mum you want to be?

- If you had a magic wand, what could you do?

- If you had all the time and the money in the world?

- What support do you need?

- What resources?

- What could you do?

- What else?

- And just one more thing?

Step 5 – action

Once you have identified what is most important to you about being a mum, you recognise your guilt triggers, you have self-appreciation for what you do and what your strengths are, and you know what you can do to make changes, it is time to take action.

You have brainstormed the different options, now think about options which are the most appealing? Which would be the quickest? The easiest?

Take just one, maybe two of those options and decide WHEN you are going to action it.

Write down WHAT you are going to do and WHEN you are going to do it:

I am going to

_____

Step 6 – reinforcement

The final stage in ditching the guilt is to identify what you can do every day to turn small changes into positive habits.

We know from the research that Maxine Harley shared that it takes on average 66 days to change your behaviour. Give yourself permission to be a beginner. If you miss a day or two, that is ok. Just get back on track as quickly as you can.

Small changes can make a good difference.

Good luck and do let me know how you get on. You can email me at srb@sherrybevan.co.uk.

Key learning points

1. Identify what is most important to YOU about being a mum.

2. Give yourself credit for what you are already doing, learn to self-appreciate.

3. Recognise your guilt triggers.

4. Establish what you want to do differently.

5. Brainstorm your options.

6. Put it into action because small changes can make a big difference.

Additional resources

The complete *Working Mum's Guide to Ditching the Guilt* is available to purchase at www.sherrybevan.co.uk/ditch-the-guilt/ as six downloadable audio modules with accompanying workbooks.

In the next section we start to explore the options for those mums who have taken a career break and are ready to go back to work or start their own business. The first story is from a mum with a dramatic start to motherhood.

How one mum's dramatic birth evolved into a career change

Naomi Martell-Bundock

They told us, 'He's trying to breathe on his own.' My husband and I looked at each other and thought, 'This must be good.' We had no idea. 'No, it's not a good thing… He's fighting against the ventilator and he needs the ventilator to help him breathe. He needs the ventilator to live.

Naomi Martell-Bundock is a wellbeing expert who helps people 'take back control' after a change in circumstances. Naomi has two boys (aged 10 and 11). Before children, she worked in the City in investment banking in organisational change. After the birth of her children, her confidence plummeted when she was plunged into the world of hospitals. The project management of her son's care evolved into a significant career change. We started with Naomi's dramatic birth story.

NMB: I was newly wed and life was good: we were expecting our first baby, we lived in a brand new house and everything was how you hope your life is going to be.

When I was six months pregnant, to be precise 25 weeks and 3 days, I was in a lot of pain. We were away for the weekend, I walked into A&E at the nearest hospital at 1.30pm and I gave birth at 2.22pm.

In that hour, life literally turned upside down. They didn't know if the baby was going to survive. And if he did, they didn't know what state he would be in. His lungs weren't working properly.

After birth, he was taken straight away so we didn't see him. When we finally had a conversation, they told us, 'He's trying to breathe on his own.' My husband and I looked at each other and thought, 'This must be good.' We had no idea. They looked at us. 'No, it's not a good thing.' How can it not be a good thing? He's trying to breathe.

They replied, 'He's fighting against the ventilator and he needs the ventilator to help him breathe. He needs the ventilator to live.' Our life closed in on us and we became numb. From that point on, we were living day to day and sometimes hour to hour. That first night we waited for several hours until they were able to come and talk to us, 'We don't know if he's going to survive. He's got a less than 40% chance.' They were trying to tell us that they didn't think he was going to live.

They had to stabilise him enough to get him to a hospital capable of coping with a baby requiring intensive care. He got blue-lighted up to Birmingham that night. Having been shown how to express my breast milk, I was transported up as an inpatient the next day.

SB: *At six months you're not prepared.*

NMB: Absolutely. We weren't prepared. We had a decorated room but nothing in it. No clothes or cot. Not that it mattered. He was in six different hospitals over five and a half months.

He survived the first few days but had a pulmonary haemorrhage [a lung bleed] in the night on day four. They worked through the night to save him. At 6.30am they said, 'We've done all that we can, we think he's ok.' We got through that. He had another operation at day 28 in another hospital. He got through that despite the new hospital trying to stop his pain-killing drugs because they hadn't read his notes.

I spent six months living in the different hospitals that he was in. My life existed within 4 walls. I was numb and submerged in a very different approach to life. My career went. It became very evident that we weren't going to be able to return to life as we knew it. When my husband and I talked, it made sense for me to stay at home and care for him. I felt that I had no choice. My new job was to project manage the support and the care. I just didn't know it at the time. I acted on auto-pilot. We had so many different consultants, so many different nurses to make sure he was having his basic needs met.

Suddenly it didn't matter if I was wearing pyjamas or getting dressed, half the time, living and sleeping in hospitals. I wasn't getting out, I wasn't seeing anybody outside of this world. When I did, I felt as if I had nothing to share, to contribute, and I felt guilty, as though I should be by the incubator side 24 hours a day.

When he finally came home, he was on oxygen, with tubes. He was fed with my expressed milk through a tube in his mouth and then his nose.

I used my skills because I had nothing else to do with my days. I wasn't conscious, just numb. I'd lost my confidence. I didn't want to see family or friends. I didn't understand who I was talking to from the medical profession and how to make it work but after a while it became evident that the professionals didn't really work together. They were supportive individually, but I was looking after a baby with many, many needs – not all of them evident at this time. It was a really difficult time. Really difficult.

My life became consumed by looking after my son. Every specialist within the NHS knew that what they were talking about was really important, but this lack of cohesion, this lack of understanding of priorities, was really hard to get my head around.

I had to value what everybody was giving me but I had to take time to reflect, 'Ok, so I'm being told this by the lung consultant and I'm being told this by the physiotherapist, this by the dietician, and this by the paediatrician,' and it went on.

There are only 24 hours in the day and I could not physically do all of it. I asked myself, 'What do I trust as being the most important thing at this moment?'

I would plan it out, usually taking my notes into meetings helped me find the strength to say, 'I've spoken to this other professional and they've suggested such and such. How would that fit with what you're suggesting to me?' It was very much about having conversations that brought those conflicting views out in the open and then we were able to make decisions to go forward.

If you are in a meeting with health professionals, and if you do end up with tears in your eyes, or even break down, it's ok. The health professional you're talking to may feel uncomfortable. They may not say anything because they don't know what to say. What I have found is that when you give yourself a moment and pull yourself back together, they realise that they are dealing with a human being and they will do everything they can to support you.

SB: *Now you run your own business as a successful coach working with individuals and small businesses. How did that change happen?*

NMB: When my son was about two or three, I was really struggling. I was on the floor. I didn't know how to manage things.

My intention had been to have my baby and six months later go back to work. We lived away from family and hadn't made friends in our new area. I'd not attended any antenatal classes because I had my baby so early. Life was bleak and barren and we didn't know what to do.

One day I took him to an osteopath – I don't know why, call it gut intuition. It meant that I was able to get out of the house. We weren't allowed to mix with other people for the first few winters because of his lung issues. In the first two years, mixing in any kind of mother and baby group would have put him at severe risk.

I was completely isolated. We had spent three weeks at our home hospital and met three other sets of parents. Once we were back home, the other parents supported me where they could. I am forever grateful to those lovely ladies and we are all friends to this day.

Otherwise, physically, I was isolated. Even if somebody turned up at the door and they had a cold or a cough, I had to say, 'I'm sorry, you can't come in.'

Anyway, when we moved area, I changed osteopath; she charged 50% more than my old osteopath, but we found the money. By then I had a second boy – there are 19 months between my children. Whenever we saw the osteopath, for the rest of the day I'd notice that I was perkier, I had more energy, and my children were happier and calmer. I started to talk to her. She was training in neurolinguistic programming (NLP), specifically in health and healing.

I decided to train, with no real expectation. Slowly it started to bring back my confidence. Now I have a true lifestyle business and it's built around the family. In the first few years I would almost resent the family, resent the children, not them but the situation. Now I know that my children are absolutely my priority: I love my children and I love being with them (I couldn't say that back then), I love my work, and I love my clients.

SB: *Was that a conscious decision to build a career around family or was it initially a personal development opportunity?*

NMB: First and foremost it was my opportunity for personal development. I did think it could evolve but I had no idea how. First I had to fix me, Sherry. My confidence didn't exist. My self-esteem was on the floor. I was functioning but I certainly wasn't living and I couldn't let that go on. The business grew organically – there was very little consciousness going on!

SB: *I'd love you to share advice or tips for those mums thinking about setting up their own business. What have you learned?*

NMB: The very first is to review all the things you have done, highlight the ones you love, the ones you enjoy, that don't feel like work and be very clear on the things that you don't like. What do you love, what don't you love, whether that is tasks or skills or types of people.

Ask yourself – why is it you want a career change and what do you want to gain from it? In my situation, it was because my circumstances had changed. Be very clear on what your circumstances are now – what will they allow you to do? – but don't be restricted by your circumstances. It's more a case of understanding how things will fit in. It's working out all your permutations.

The other thing: is being your own boss what you want? What does it mean? When you are your own boss, when you start out, you do everything. You are Chief Cook and Bottle Washer all at once. It's not for everybody.

My best advice is to get a huge amount of paper and brainstorm or mindmap it. I'm a big 'paper and pen, draw it all out' person.

Paper and pen really frees you up to get the juices flowing and to think outside the box. You can put the neat version on your computer and print it out later if you want an easier format to refer to.

Once you are in that career change, let it evolve. Be flexible. Be available for opportunities. Be clear and focused.

SB: *I love the 'let it evolve' philosophy – so powerful. That's certainly true for my own business. I come from a technology background and spent the first two years focused on working with non-lawyers in law firms. However I've always worked with women too. In the last six months, my business has evolved so that now I specialise in working with women who are at the crossroads after children.*

NMB: Another thing that I want to share is to be really clear that *there are no rules*. You can let it evolve but you've got to be able to find the strength to be able to cope with that. If you struggle without rules, it can give you an extra pressure that maybe you don't need.

It's also vital to discuss your desires with your husband or partner if you have one. Our partners want to support us, so share your thoughts. Together you can work out a way that makes it work for you as an individual, and you as a family.

SB: *What are the main differences between working for a large organisation, versus running your own business?*

NMB: I worked in big corporations in teams where different people did different things. Somebody booked my meetings, somebody would write up my notes, or submit my expenses. When you run your own business, you do it all yourself. That's a biggie to get your head around and manage your time effectively.

I don't have the capacity to go from being parent to book-keeper to delivering the wellbeing coaching, the bit that I'm best at. I made a promise at the beginning that other than using our money for the initial training, I haven't borrowed a penny of our money.

I've always made my money in the business before I've spent it. Now, that was a conscious choice. I made it out of respect for my husband and myself. That's very different from working in a big company when the money is always there. You might have to ask for it, and put in a budget proposal, but the money is there.

You decide on your values – that's one of the differences. You're creating the environment and the culture; not fitting into a pre-existing one.

When you're working for a company you're used to a regular pay packet. You know that money is going to come in every month regardless. It's not like that when you start a business. Be clear on how you're going to manage that, because if you end up with financial issues on top of trying to build your business, that makes things hard. Doing things from a position of stress to the point of desperation, you're going to struggle.

I essentially earn one year and save what I will pay myself the following year. I know how much I'm going to be paying myself this year because I earned it all last year. It means we know exactly what's coming. Taking that approach has made such a difference, a really positive change. I've been told by many people that I'm the first person they know of to take this empowered approach.

This is my fourth year trading as a limited company. Before that I was self-employed for six years. I deliver, I do the work but I have a technical Virtual Assistant and a Personal Assistant (one of the mums at school who wanted work to fit around her three young children). I use a book-keeper, she's another mum from school. What I'm doing has grown, evolved on its own. I always wanted my business to empower my clients AND the people who work with me.

SB: That fits with Loral Langemeier's philosophy of giving work to other people. By outsourcing some of the
work, you avoid working 24 hours a day and it's good
for the economy and for other people.

It almost brings you full circle, starting out when your
son was born early, to now being able to give work to
others. I think that's beautiful.

Key learning points

1. When you set up a business, it is ok to let it evolve
   over time.

2. There are no rules.

3. Before you start, understand why you want to start
   your own business and what you want to gain.

4. Start by reviewing all your skills; highlight the ones
   you love, be very clear on what you don't like.

5. If you have a husband or partner, be open with them
   and discuss your thoughts so that you can really
   make a success of work and love.

Additional resources

BLISS – charity supporting parents of babies born too
soon, too small or too sick: www.bliss.org.uk/.

TOMMY's – funding research into stillbirth, premature birth
and miscarriage, and providing information for parents-to-
be: www.tommys.org/.

If you are thinking about starting your own business join Sherry's 12-week **Stepping Stones** course: www.sherry-bevan.co.uk/stepping-stones/.

Naomi talked about identifying the reasons for a career change, and what is important to you. In the next interview, Nicola Mullarkey continues this by exploring how to understand our core values before contemplating a career change.

Understand your core values to help with a career change

Nicola Mullarkey

I booked the flights. He didn't talk to me for 24 hours.

Nicola Mullarkey is The Honest Recruiter. She has been in recruitment for 17 years and works with small businesses and solopreneurs to help them find the right people for their business. She uses a seven-step recruitment process in which step one is Working Out Your Values.

Identifying and understanding your values will enable you to build your life, business or career around those values so that you feel happier and more fulfilled.

Nicola started by explaining the concept of values and core values.

NM: The Oxford English Dictionary defines 'values' as principles or standards of behaviour, one's judgement of what is important in life. Your internal beliefs or your belief system guides you in how you behave, your actions and how you live your life. That's how I define core values. The core values are what make us as a person. Values are intangibles such as freedom, creativity, integrity, trust, expertise.

SB: *If we're not sure of our core values, how do we work these out?*

NM: Think about a time when you've got really angry or had a really strong emotion; when you've got really upset about something. It's likely that something's happened or somebody has asked you to break one of your core values.

The first time that I identified that trust was one of my core values was when a client questioned it. I have a strong emotion connected with trust. I had delivered some CVs to a client. She came back saying that they'd been talking to another agency and this agency had sent the CV first. I was fine with that. Then I had a conversation with the candidate and I discovered we were first. However the client disbelieved me and honestly, I could feel the adrenaline pump around my body. I felt my face go red, I could barely talk. I said another three or four words to terminate the call politely. I had to get up from my desk and walk away because I was so angry, not at her, but that she was questioning what I'd said; questioning my integrity.

It was resolved, and she knew that I was not lying, however it is interesting when somebody questions one of your core beliefs – I saw red. That very rarely happens. It isn't just when you feel anger, it's strong emotions.

Once you have your top six or so, you can work on them to identify which three are your core values. Usually you have a gut instinct.

NM: You might be wondering about the benefits of knowing your core values. You know those days when everything is going right; it's flowing and you love everything you are doing. Living your core values is having that all the time. You're not having those moments where you get really angry.

When I feel that somebody is questioning me, I can take a step back and reflect, 'That's my core value.' I can understand that they are not questioning my value or me, it's how they look at things.

As a business, when you work with other people, whether outsourcing or employing, if you don't have a business culture aligned to your values, you will end up working with people who will break your core values. That will bring out strong emotions and you might end up hating it.

If you're looking for a job, you want to ensure that you are ticking all your boxes. If you are working in a highly competitive environment but competition isn't something that you value, will you truly be satisfied in that role? Knowing your core values helps in so many areas of your life.

SB: *What are the signs that you're not being true to your core values? How do we know if our core values are out of alignment with our employer, or our business?*

NM: Have you ever felt a niggle that something's not quite right, or someone's asked you to do something and you think, 'I feel a bit uncomfortable with that.'? They're asking you to do something against one of your values. It might not be a core value. If they ask you to do something and you respond, 'No way would I do that,' that's a core value.

SB: *The difference is that the core values are the unbreakable values?*

NM: Definitely. They're your beliefs that you don't want to cross. It wouldn't even enter your head, you wouldn't ever consider doing it.

SB: *Presumably then, it wouldn't enter your head that anybody else would consider doing it either. You might be blind in that area of your life.*

NM: Very much so – knowing your core values makes you realise where your blind spots are.

If you're working in a job or doing something that you're not happy with, you'll feel it. You'll feel the energy being sucked out of you, you'll dread going into the office because you're not in your flow. That's the only way I can word it.

SB: *Running this conference, talking to amazing people and seeing everybody taking actions forward, I feel fantastic. I'm in my flow and very much working to my values. Sometimes, you might have that niggle and unhappiness at work. How would you know whether it's the job, the environment or the employer? It could be that it's not about making a career change, maybe it's the employer; their values are not in alignment with yours.*

NM: You may be able to work in a different way so that you don't need to change your job. It's powerful when you realise how you're working and why people are doing things the way they do them. Understanding your values is not the answer to everything. Knowing your values is a powerful way to identify that this company might not be for you.

SB: *If you work with somebody whose values are drastically different, will you get on with that person or is it a disaster waiting to happen?*

NM: You might get on well for a short period of time. If you're working on a major project, I believe that you will butt heads because you will be coming from different angles. You won't be looking at a common goal. You'll be wanting to deliver different things.

SB: *One of my current clients, her boss is brought into companies to make them more efficient and more successful. He sacks people and changes processes. For him, achievement is undoubtedly a key driver. Whereas if you are a midwife, achievement is unlikely to be a core value.*

My husband and I clash over things but at the foundation of our partnership, our core values are similar. If your core values are very different to your partner's, that relationship is likely to be fire and ice. Fantastic perhaps in the first two or three years.

NM: Indeed. The first time I broke one of my husband's core values, I thought I was doing something lovely. He is from Australia and his parents are over there.

We'd just missed his Dad's 80th birthday and I managed to get some cheap flights to go over. We had been talking about it for four or five days, and I said, 'It's a few days after your Dad's birthday but we can still go over.' He said 'I really like that idea.' In the morning, I got a quote and he said, 'That's really good. Let me think about it.'

We got on with our day and at lunch time I said, 'OK, I want to book the tickets. I said I'd get back to her by lunchtime.' He said 'Oh, I was thinking about it.' 'I've given you four hours. Come on, it will be really great.'

I spoke to one of our friends who said, 'His parents will love to see you.' I booked the flights. He didn't talk to me for 24 hours.

It was six months before we were getting married. He doesn't make quick decisions and he needs to think things through. It took us six months to choose our TV, which has lasted for years but he had to see it and touch it. His values are different to mine in that one area. I learnt that the hard way. He was really pleased that we went to Australia, but he didn't like being forced to make a decision really quickly.

SB: *Many would have thought that was a romantic gesture but it backfired on you.*

NM: It did. I got the silent treatment.

SB: *Let's summarise. If we're not being true to our core values, we will notice the 'niggles' and not feel totally happy. What else might we be feeling or seeing?*

NM: If you're consistently not aligned to your core values, it will eventually manifest and you'll become ill.

SB: *If you love what you do, and you're working in alignment with your core values, you are passionate, full of energy.*

NM: Yes, and people see the energy. They'll see you're buzzing.

SB: *How do we make sure that our career will fit our core values?*

NM: If you're looking for another job, most businesses share their values, certainly the larger ones. However just because they share what their values are as a company, it doesn't necessarily mean they live it. Do some research, ask around. Are they living their values? Do they work in the same way as their values? Talk to people that have left the company to understand what's it like and why did they leave?

If a company is not 100% aligned to your core values, it's not the be-all and end-all. What is the difference and are you happy with that compromise? It's having an open mind and being aware.

SB: *Perhaps find other ways within that role or within that company. If creativity is a core value and the company has very structured ways of working, you can take your creativity outside work?*

NM: Even if it is structured, it doesn't mean that you can't be yourself within the structure. Often businesses are happy for people to come forward with ideas. If you are creative and you come up with ideas, put them forward.

Use your values to consider what type of job you should pursue, or what type of business to go into. If you're not driven by delivery or sales, you don't want to go into a sales-oriented role. If you're very caring and nurturing, where can you use those skills? How can you use those skills to deliver a service aligned to your values?

If you're being authentic in everything you do, you don't have to put on a different face to go into work or a different face to talk to your friends. You can be yourself. You don't have to change your persona and waste energy.

SB: *Therefore less stressful. Authenticity matters and it is about understanding your core values.*

If you are thinking about changing career or setting up your own business, you can think back to moments in your life where you have been in that zone where you've said, 'Throw it at me, I can deal with it.' When you felt that unstoppable energy. Identify what exactly you were doing to make you feel like that: how can you use that again to set up your own business?

For example, one of my recent clients was on a career break – in our sessions, she talked about how she was on the top of the world when she was organis- ing the school summer fair. Working through it, she realised that she loves organising and bringing teams of people together. It wasn't what she'd done before children. She was able to figure out what she loved and was able to take that passion and present her event management experience to a future employer.

NM: She looked at the skills and not the job she was doing. It's worth sitting down with a pen and paper and identifying those 'in the flow' moments. What is it that you are good at that you've not thought about aligning to a job or work?

SB: *Understand those moments when you have that 'bouncy' feeling, and identify what exactly you are doing in those moments to pinpoint the skills you are using.*

NM: And replicate it.

SB: *Gay Hendricks in* The Big Leap *talks about your Zone of Excellence and your Zone of Genius. Excellence is when you're very good at something: you're effective and efficient. The Zone of Genius is when you're doing something and it's no effort. 12 hours go by and you thought you've just sat down.*

How do you convince a prospective employer that we have these skills, if you've not done it within a work environment?

NM: Present examples. Do some voluntary work or something on the side where you can prove it. Emphasise where you've used those skills: what did you do? What were the results?

SB: *Thank you so much Nicola. In conclusion, if you identify your core values, it can make a huge difference.*

If you're unhappy with work, with life in general, or if you're having regular conflicts with somebody that you work with, understanding where you're both coming from can make a huge difference.

Key learning points

1. Identify your core values.

2. Authenticity matters: be.

3. Identify your 'in flow' skills.

4. Present examples to potential employers.

Additional resources

Visit **www.theconfidentmother.co.uk/book/extras** for a downloadable PDF file for a quick and easy method to identify your personal core values.

Once you identify your core values, you may well come to the conclusion that setting up your own business from home is the right move for you. In which case, you'll love Sarah Buchanan-Smith's advice in the next interview.

Setting up your own business from home

Sarah Buchanan-Smith

'No' might mean, 'No, not now, maybe later,' but 'No' can mean 'No, not ever.' If you never follow up, you'll never find out.

Sarah Buchanan-Smith is the Kitchen Table Consultant. She helps women with professional backgrounds set up their own consultancy businesses based at home, which is exactly what Sarah has done herself. She is the epitome of the wildly left-wing rebel at university who was going to change the world and ended up working in an investment bank. After children she returned to the corporate world for a while, and then set up her own business making good use of her skills on a wide range of inspiring projects. Sarah feels strongly that women have incredible skills but often struggle with how to use these from home. She shares her five steps to setting up your business at home so that you don't waste the professional skills and experience you already have.

SBS: The **first step** is to ask yourself, '**Do I really want to do this?**'

A flexible business based at home using your professional skills sounds wonderful in theory however it is hard work. I want to make that clear. Not to put you off, but to take a reality check because at the beginning it is hard work. You have to put the hours in. It's exciting and it's motivating; you're doing something you passionately love. But it is **hard** work.

Consider the unpredictability as well. Can you put up with not knowing where your first client is going to come from? Some months, I've had five clients and the next month none. At first I didn't understand that you have to nurture your 'pipeline'. It will be uncertain and unpredictable to start with, which can seem over-whelming, but it gets better. It's a learning curve and you have to learn how to manage your time. Every-body can cope with unpredictability; it's whether you want to.

Setting boundaries – one of the things that I had to learn is the art of saying 'no' to potential clients, which can be quite scary. You have to say, 'No, not now,' if you physically cannot take on another client. Can you say 'no'? It's really important because you're doing this for a reason: to spend more time with your kids, or to have more time to yourself. Saying 'no' is empowering. When you say 'no', explain why and when you can help them. However it's good for your image, if you are in a position to say 'no'.

One of the things about running your business is that it can get addictive. You're always on. It is important to say 'no', not only to other people but to keep your-self in check.

The second step takes the longest and can be the most frustrating. It's where mums can get lost:

recognising your skills and working out how to use those skills. This is where the fun begins. What can I do with my life? How can I use my skills? Strip back your labels and look at the skills you have, both work experience and softer skills.

If you want to be a consultant, spend time to work out the areas you'd like to work in. I went from investment banking to fundraising consultant. It's exciting to work out how to use your skills, not only in the work you do but the area that you want to work in. It takes time, but it's worth spending a few weeks working out where you want to go.

SB: *What's the best way to identify your skills and strip back the labels?*

SBS: I'm a qualified accountant so you get the spreadsheet answer from me: take a piece of paper and get it all out of your head. Take your CV and distil it down to your core skills. If you've written down 'risk management', unpack that into the actual things you do. Think about the big experiences that you've had or that you've helped people through.

SB: *I often suggest a mind map to my clients.*

SBS: A brilliant way to do it. Build up a picture of your skills. When you know what skills you have, it's important to look at how you want to live your life. You are making this big change for a reason.

What is important to you? For me, it was flexibility. Write all these things on your piece of paper or your mind map. You're dreaming up your perfect business at this point. You may have 10 or 15 different business ideas running around in your head so it's helpful to have that piece of paper to act as an anchor. It can get overwhelming, so for each business idea, ask: do I have the skills? Will it fit with my values and the way I want to live my life?

The next step is **what to charge**. So many get stuck on this point and it's worth working out upfront. You need to have that figure in mind before you start looking for clients because it guides you down the right path. You could search the internet and find out what your competitors are doing. However in the consulting world it's difficult to find rates online, so you need to work it out yourself.

My fee calculator is a formula that works out how much you want to earn, taking into account the business costs, how many weeks you want to work in a year, how many days a week you want to work, how many hours a day you can work. It sounds complicated but it's simply plugging numbers into a calculator. Think about how much time you will be generating income vs working **on** your business. It is important to come up with a realistic rate.

If you're working in a specialist sector or a niche market, you may already have a feel for what might be an acceptable figure. Often consultants charge more than you realise.

If you come out with a rate of £800 a day, that's fine, you have a starting point. If somebody wants a piece of work doing tomorrow, you can charge a premium. Or offer a heavily discounted rate to a charity. You can play around with your fees.

SBS: **The final step is where to find your clients**. It's a simple answer and I know it annoys people when I give it to them. Basically, go out and talk to people. There is no magic formula. When I first set up my business, I talked to other consultants. I took people out for lunch, for dinner and coffees. I go to lots of networking events, not random networking, events that have my target clients.

The follow-up process is key. You can't expect to give somebody your business card and transform them immediately into clients. It's about relationship-building. Sometimes it can take six weeks, two months before you get into a position to work with them.

When you go to networking events, come out with a business card. Not everybody you meet is a potential client but they might be helpful to you in some other way. They might be doing something interesting in their business that you can learn from. Be patient.

Keep track of all your contacts. A simple Excel spreadsheet is fine at the start. Keep it simple. Follow up. Only 10% or 20% of people that go to networking events follow up with people they met. Such a waste of effort. Send an email saying, 'Really nice to meet you,' follow up and get a strategy meeting or a call where you can add value.

You need to be tenacious but there's the art of knowing when to stop. 'No' might mean, 'No, not now, maybe later,' but 'No' can mean, 'No, not ever.' If you never follow up, you'll never find out.

SB: *If you're working in a particular niche, you already have good contacts.*

SBS: Exactly. I built my network from zero. I took out everyone I knew in Edinburgh who was running her own business. I hated it at first. I was scared but I just did it. Once you've done it a couple of times, you realise that they're quite flattered to be asked. It's a win-win situation.

It is hard work. Stick with it because the rewards are so fantastic. You have to get your head down for six months to a year to get it up and running properly.

SB: *Sarah, I've really enjoyed talking to you today. It's been fascinating to hear your perspective on setting up your own business.*

Key learning points

1. Get yourself ready.

2. Build the foundations.

3. Identify what you really want to do with your skills.

4. Work out your value in the market.

5. Find your first client.

Additional resources

If you are a busy mum who dreams of setting up her own business, you will love my **Stepping Stones** 12-week course. Build confidence and develop the know-how to start your own business. Find out more at www.sherrybevan.co.uk/stepping-stones/.

What if… what if you are running your own business, what if you are back at work, what if it just feels all too much? How do you deal with the overwhelm? In the next interview, Julia Harris shows us how to get balance in our lives.

How to manage that elusive work-life-family balance

Julia Harris

There's no such thing as time management, it's self-management... Self-management is the difference between success and failure when it comes to work-life balance.

Julia Harris first started coaching as part of her job when she worked as an Operational Manager for the Civil Service. She now works as a success coach, helping people, mostly women and mostly mums who are struggling to do it all, to put themselves first and find the time to do everything they want to do. Julia works with women who want more from life but have the feeling that they're not good enough, which fits in so beautifully with the overall theme of The Confident Mother.

Julia shared her six-step iPower formula to a better work-life balance.

JH: For me work-life balance is a very small part of what you do. I want people to start thinking differently about the 'can you have it all' debate.

The world is full of overwhelm. Things aren't going to change. We're never going back to that time where many women didn't work. There wasn't the rushing around that we do now, all the school clubs, emails at all times of day and night, there wasn't social media to cause distractions.

People think overwhelm is a dirty word, but it's a fact of life. We're constantly bombarded with messages and we think we have to keep up with it.

I like to think of work-life balance differently. You might go through stages where you are overwhelmed. But it's about balancing the times when you are overwhelmed and making sure you have the recovery times. If we put our body under stress constantly with little recovery time, we get burned out or become ill. The recovery time is essential. It's not a constantly balanced life. Some people might like the hectic life. Some people need more downtime. It's whatever feels right to the individual. There's no judgement about what is or isn't the right balance to have.

The foundational step to a more successful life starts with tuning into the real you, the authentic you, getting **in tune with your identity**.

When we are mothers we very easily can lose that sense of identity. We become a mother and that is how people see us. We get labelled.

When we get in tune with who we are as an individual, we can make healthier decisions and then we are a better role model for our children. We might always put our children first, but we must take care of ourselves and tune in with who **we** are. Therefore we are teaching our children to do things in a different way when they become parents. If you want to bring up healthy, happy children in the world, teach them to be an individual and to respect boundaries from the start. Sometimes that's easier said than done, but it's important to have that time for you.

I talk about mums, women in general, as the cornerstone of their home. Everything fits around them. The cornerstone is the first brick laid in the building and it sets the level for everything else. If you become a doormat or you are always at the beck and call of people, if you don't set boundaries from the start, if you don't find time for yourself, you're teaching people how to treat you. You're not the most effective person you can be. Find time for you, and you will be more creative and more effective, and a better role model.

The second step is **planning**. Planning what you truly want, thinking about the long-term vision, and how you want your children to see you. It may be difficult when they're young. What sort of boundaries do you want to set in place when they're older? Sometimes we give into the tantrums because it's easier to say 'yes'. But long term, how do you want your children to learn from you?

Plan in the time for you. I start with a year plan. I work from home, for myself. The first thing that goes in my diary is my time off; it might be time for me, or time with the family. I plan in the days off for myself or the days that I want with my children. I plan in little chunks of time for recharging my batteries such as going for a walk along the beach. If you're self-employed, you are your most important client; if you're a mum with a busy family, you are the cornerstone. Plan in your time and treat it as important: it might be family time, or time alone. Yes, be flexible, but make sure you plan in that time, otherwise you drift along.

Whether you're working, or self-employed, you'll be more effective if you plan and take time off.

The next thing in the iPower is **overwhelm**. Overwhelm is a fact of life now. It can lead us into a negative downward spiral and we end up stressed, frustrated, upset, angry, and not feeling good about life in general.

However we can recognise the signs of overwhelm. For me it's getting snappy with the kids or when I start biting my nails. When I was working, one of the signs of a stressful day was getting home and reaching for a glass of wine.

It didn't mean I had a drinking problem but it was a coping mechanism. The harder and the more difficult I found that job, the more and more I was reaching for that glass of wine. It was a signal for me to unwind, hearing the bottle open and the clink of the glass.

I learned that you can change that and you can find a different way to respond, whether it's a bath, locking yourself in the loo and having a scream; whatever works for you. If you can recognise your overwhelm signs, you can do something about it.

Learn to recognise your triggers too. Take action to calm yourself down before you go into that stressful situation. Find your coping strategies.

SB: *What's your favourite coping strategy, Julia?*

JH: A walk along the beach. I feel so much better when I get back and I'm much more productive after I've taken time out. That might take an hour out of my day. There are other things I can do in 30 seconds, such as some deep breathing which resets the stress hormones running around in my body. If you have 10 minutes, maybe meditation or mindfulness. Whatever time you have, you can do things at your desk in 10 minutes or less.

Sometimes we think they're so simple we don't do them. The simplest things are the easiest to do. Make them a habit and recognise the signs. You don't want to get to the stage where you're pulling out your hair or crying in the loo. Put them into your life before you get to that critical stage.

'W' is the **work-life balance**. Sometimes we think we need to be better at managing our time. I say there's no such thing as time management, it's about self-management. We all have the same 24 hours. It is about self-management: that's why the identity is important; that's why the planning is important, that's why the overwhelm strategies are important. Self-management makes the difference between success and failure when it comes to work-life balance.

Get over the need to juggle and multi-task. Sometimes we need to. But there are times when we have to give something our absolute focus, whether it's at work, or spending quality time with the children. When we try to do five things at once, we end up doing nothing effectively.

Do one thing at a time. I can't focus for two hours at a time so I build breaks in. Find a way of staying focused on one thing at a time. Stop trying to do five things at once. Take control of your inbox, especially if you work in an office environment or work from home. If you love your social media, take charge of it. Don't let it overwhelm your life.

I used to go into work, and I'd have 70 emails before I even started. I'd be stressed just looking at them.

Start setting boundaries. If your boss gives you something else to do, say, 'I have these five tasks and I have time to do three of them. Which three do you want me to prioritise?' Start having those difficult conversations with people.

What happened before we had email? We're expected to be on call all the time and that leads to overwhelm. Set up those boundaries and stick to them. Lead by example. The world has to change. Value your time. Respect your time.

If you put everybody else's needs before your own, you'll probably get it all done but you go home and shout at the kids. This happened to me and I made myself ill.

Then we have 'e' for **energy management**. As busy mothers we don't think about preserving our energy. There are things that we need to do to manage our energy but there are things that drain our mental energy: the little things that we are tolerating; somebody treating us in a poor way; disorganised mornings trying to get the kids ready for school. They may be little things, but they drain our energy.

For many of my clients, the morning routine crops up a lot. Too busy in the evening to sort out the school uniforms; they don't have time to make lunches, so they try to do it all in the morning. We end up stressed to bits, then we take that stress to work with us. If you have a long commute, that adds to the stress too.

What little things can you do? Start with something as simple as knowing where your keys are in the morning. One client had a very stressful job and could never find her keys.

Sometimes, we get so overwhelmed, we think we have to make massive changes. I could have put small changes in place sooner and not made myself ill. It got out of hand and there was no going back for me. I thought I needed to make a huge change and I couldn't do that. I knew the job was sucking the life out of me but I didn't think I could leave. Ultimately I had to for my health. Sometimes it's the simplest things that can make a big difference.

JH: The 'r' in iPower is about **relationships**. Not just relationships with a loved one, it could be relationships with a colleague or your mother-in-law. Some relationships aren't serving us as well as they could. It may be that you don't get on with that person or they irritate the life out of you.

Think differently about those relationships – relationships are another thing that we tolerate. We can change the relationship by having less of our negative attachment to it, whether it's talking to that person, whether it's understanding that they have a different perspective. It might be that we need to talk and connect more. A better relationship leads into the work-life balance.

To me, the relationship aspect tops it all off: your identity and the planning is the foundation. The overwhelm strategies, the work life-balance strategies, and the energy strategies are what we need to put in place to keep things going. Then we can look at the relationships.

We may need to forgive an ex-husband and understand that we're never going to have a perfect relationship; we're never going to see eye to eye but we can agree to stop arguing in front of the kids. There's common ground that can be found if you take responsibility for your end of that relationship. You can do your bit so you feel you've done as much as you can.

It changes the dynamics and you feel more in control of the situation and your feelings.

We can't always control the outcome but we can control how we feel about it. People often want a magic solution for work-life balance. Being balanced is a state of mind. It's feeling happy, content, and at peace, so that you can deal with the overwhelm.

JH: It's about not having judgement nor comparing your-selves to others, when you don't know what's going on behind the scenes. Just because somebody looks to have balance in their life, it doesn't mean that they're happy. We need to check in with our feelings more and if it feels good, do more of it. We're all different, we find that balance in different ways.

JH: We are in different times now and we need to live life differently, yet we still compare ourselves to people with different values and different beliefs.

SB: *I love your emphasis on accepting that there will be times of overwhelm, and the trick is to balance these with recovery time.*

Key learning points

1. Ensure you balance the times of overwhelm with recovery times.

2. Identify your overwhelm triggers.

3. Have a list of coping strategies that you can dip into as you need them.

4. What are you tolerating? Do something about it.

5. What small changes can you make?

When you are running a small business, there are many skills and qualities that you need to nurture; the same skills and qualities that Emma Sargent believes we need to nurture in our teenagers.

Think of your teenagers as entrepreneurs

Emma Sargent

We need to make sure that we teach our teenagers to be self-sufficient; too many of them feel entitled.

Emma Sargent runs The Extraordinary Coaching Company, which helps people make money from their expertise. Recently the business partnered with Loral Langemeier to bring her financial and business education to the UK. Emma is a business coach, speaker, and author of three parenting books. Mum to two teenagers herself, Emma shares her thoughts on how the skills you need to nurture in your teenager are the same as those required of any successful entrepreneur.

ES: I don't mind if my children are entrepreneurs or not. People don't need to be entrepreneurs. I want my children to be happy and have choice. There's a lot in our culture that eradicates choice. I've got two teenagers; two completely different children. They have been my greatest teachers and I am enormously proud of them both.

Our son had a very relaxed attitude to school and school work. He didn't do A-levels, he did BTECs instead, and I was not happy about that at first. There are many more study choices now for children than when I was at school. There are different paths open. There's not a wrong path or a right path, there is a path that is right for your children. I believe in putting experiences in front of them.

When we started going to entrepreneur conferences in the States, the children were about eight or nine. They run a conference for teens. Two years ago we realised, 'If we don't take them this year, we'll never take them,' because we'll get caught up in GCSEs and A-levels. We bit the bullet and off we went. We were in a conference with 800 people and the kids were in a conference with 27. They had four days learning how to build, market and grow a business.

They had to do a Dragon's Den presentation at the end. They were the only British children and the American children were fighting over them because they wanted them to be their presenters, with their English accents.

They made lots of friends and they all connect regularly, which I find amazing. What might happen because of those connections in years to come?

We met Loral because she was a speaker. She said, 'If you come to my workshop you can bring your teenagers for free.' We had a holiday in Los Angeles and we took them to the 'Three Days to Cash' workshop.

Our daughter has an amazing work ethic. She's bright, she's focused, works hard and wants to be a lawyer. During 'Three Days to Cash', she was in a permanent state of high anxiety because essentially it is about selling. It was very uncomfortable for her. However, once she had made her first sale, a chocolate cake recipe, she was like a different child. What she learned will hold her in fabulous stead for the rest of her life.

Meanwhile our son is a demon salesman; he sold three songs which he then had to deliver (another stress level for me). He came alive. It made me relax about school. I encourage him to work hard but it makes you realise that everybody is good at something. We have to encourage them to have the choices that will make them happy. What we need to encourage in our teenagers are the qualities that adult entrepreneurs need.

Children need to learn how to have a vision. I sat the children down a few years ago and we created vision boards, cutting and sticking pictures from magazines. Our daughter refers to her vision often though she has changed things. When she created it, she was certain she was going to be a vet. One day she decided she didn't want to be a vet and for a couple of days, she didn't know what she wanted instead. She said, 'It's making me feel wobbly. I had my whole life planned out and now I don't want that.'

It was a valuable lesson – you need to be able to change your vision and for that to be ok for you.

We need to make sure that we teach our teenagers to be self-sufficient; too many of them feel entitled, encouraged by the fact that you can very easily go into debt. They see we buy things with plastic, they see their parents going into debt, they see people consuming all the time. I don't think a proper work ethic is something that is taught.

There are so many distractions now and we need to teach our teenagers about focus. If they don't focus on something, they're going to be disappointed because they won't get what they want. My son said to me often, 'I want good grades', but he took no action. It's not surprising that you don't get good grades if you don't focus.

Another skill that you need as an entrepreneur or teenager is **problem solving**. Tim and I created problems at home with work, work, work. We didn't separate work from life. It was easier to do the washing up and the cooking ourselves because we felt bad about not spending time with the kids. We didn't ask them to contribute to the home. Children need to be brought up as part of a team. Otherwise when they get to be a teenager and you do start asking them to do stuff, it comes as a surprise.

We create problems that make them dependent and continue to be dependent when they should be working towards independence. Our son is an expert at getting everybody else to think for him and do stuff for him. He's brilliant at it; he's gorgeous and charming. I'm sure it's going to work for him in the future but in the meantime I'm thinking this has got to change.

Of course trying to change it when he's nearly 17 is more difficult than if we had not rescued him from not remembering his PE kit or his art project earlier. I wish we hadn't done that. You get into patterns, and into a negative spiral if you're not careful.

We need to teach our children how to solve problems by helping them to come up with solutions rather than providing the solution ourselves. Allow them to make mistakes and to learn from those mistakes. I believe that some of the things that we have done with our son made him less confident than he might otherwise be.

I remember reading Carol Dweck's book and being devastated because we overpraise in a nonspecific way. Descriptive praise is fantastic. However it's never too late. Praise your children for working hard, for the qualities that you want them to demonstrate more often.

Another skill that we need to teach our children is financial independence and literacy. How many parents know how to explain compound interest? How many people understand that if you put something for a £100 on a credit card and you leave it for a year it turns into X amount? When your child leaves home at 18, they need to know what is involved when they buy a car. They need to know how to open a bank account. It's very important.

I'm a great believer in alternative education to find ways to put your children into situations that will educate them in skills that will stand them in good stead in life. We were lucky to be able to take them to America twice in one year but there are lots of entre-preneurial things that you can join in in this country. There are books, podcasts, online stories of young people who've done amazing things.

Teenagers can put themselves on a website like Fiv-err where they can pick up small jobs for $5. There are plenty of jobs within their range of skills that they can charge people for. Spend an hour a day doing those and it soon adds up, a better rate than working in the local pub.

A teenager can make money online. Give it a go and if you're persistent, it will work. If you're not, it won't. We have to encourage persistence. As parents, we can be guilty of molly-coddling our children away from obstacles. Yet failure is inevitable on the path to success. If you understand that, it is easier to man-age your emotional state and how you respond when failures do come your way.

We need to help our children believe that failure is fine as long as they move on and learn from it. We protect them from failing in small ways but if you learn that failure is ok in small ways, when it happens in a big way it's not so bad.

Open communication is so vital. Talk to them about everything, ask their opinions, share your opinions, discuss what's going on. I think that the level of lack of self-confidence is higher than it has ever been.

I'm grateful that my children do talk to me and share things. I've always tried to keep communication open. Whatever they tell me, I am very measured in my response because of the balance between teaching them what's ok and what's not ok. At the end of the day, you are their moral compass so they know what's right and wrong.

Yes, there are skills for life that I think we need to teach our teenagers which then give them the choice to build a business or not.

- Having a vision

- Being able to set goals and plan

- Demonstrating commitment and being persistent

- Learning from failure and mistakes

- Good communication skills

I want to end with a story which I find extraordinary. My cousin, who is much younger than me, told me that she recently got a receptionist job for which there were 200 applicants. She was the only one who looked in the interviewer's eyes and shook his hand. They told her that's why she got the job.

It's so important to be able to communicate effectively and have good manners. So many things are online, however we need to teach our children good manners and face-to-face contact stuff. Insist that you have meal times without phones as a family. I readily admit we let that slip and I'm glad that we've brought it back because it's crucial.

SB: *I love that so many of those skills that you need to run a business are the skills that we need to encourage our teenagers to develop.*

Key learning points

1. The skills you need to nurture as an entrepreneur are the same skills that you need to nurture in your teenagers.

2. Open communication is essential to build ongoing relationships with your teenager.

3. Praise your children for working hard, for the qualities that you want them to demonstrate more often.

4. Don't do everything for your teenagers. Encourage them to solve their own problems.

What if your experience of motherhood is different? For some mums, their experience of bringing up children is not quite what they expected; whether they have a child with special needs, whether they adopted, whether they are a single mum. The next two interviews tell the stories of two inspirational mums.

The mum who adopted

Somebody in the waiting room asked me, 'Did you drop him then?' I wished the ground would swallow me up.

Carole Arnold and I first met in an online antenatal group 11 years ago when we were both pregnant: me with my second child and Carole with her first. Carole is one of my heroines because her journey through motherhood is very special. She now works as an Adoption Champion for PACT, help-ing parents work their way through the adoption process. Carole has two children, George who is ten and Libby who is six. She has the same worries, concerns and guilt that any mother has, no matter her journey into motherhood. Carole starts by introducing herself before moving on to share her journey of becoming a mother.

CA: What makes us special and sometimes a bit different to the outside world is that both my children have Down's syndrome. The other thing that defines me as a mum is that George is a birth child and Libby is adopted. I've come to motherhood in lots of different ways.

We talk about George as being my first child but I was pregnant before George. I had a traumatic early miscarriage almost exactly 11 years ago. Somewhat against my better judgement, I fell pregnant again very quickly. I took a lot of grief and worry with me into the second pregnancy. The early weeks of my pregnancy with George were scary because I was waiting for something to go wrong. My first experience was that things go wrong and you have a funeral at the end of it.

11 years ago there weren't routine early pregnancy scans. My husband and I paid for an early scan – not wanting the test results but because we needed to see that baby on the scan.

The consultant gave us the results: a 1 in 5,715 chance of having a baby with Down's syndrome. I had a routine 20-week scan when they did start to find things. They diagnosed George with bilateral talipes (clubbed feet). While we were still pregnant, we were able to meet the orthopaedic consultant who would treat our baby when it was born so he could explain the treatment. My negative attitude wasn't fading because this scan had shown something wrong.

They kept picking up little things: a short femur measurement, an unusual blood pressure in an umbilical artery… the list kept growing. My pregnancy continued and I was beginning to calm down. At Christmas, I was 36 weeks pregnant. I was at the top of the stairs, fainted, and fell a short way.

I was admitted to hospital and 48 hours later George arrived. It was a shock. I'd been preparing myself for the fact that this pregnancy wasn't going to end in a baby. Then it happened so quickly and with an emergency caesarean at 36 weeks. I was lying on the bed in recovery knowing that I'd delivered a little boy and knowing that he was going straight to special care. My midwife popped her head round the door and said, 'Did you know he's got Down's syndrome?' and popped back out again. I remember so clearly laying there and thinking, wow these drugs are really good you can hallucinate all sorts of things.

I thought I'd had a crazy dream because nobody would tell you your baby had Down's syndrome in that way. 48 hours later, when George was two days old, a paediatric consultant sat Keith and me down. He explained that they'd done genetic screening, which confirmed that George had Down's syndrome.

It was just such a shock. When you look back, all the indicators were there. Somebody should have picked it up. But nobody had. We sat there in Special Care. I hadn't been able to hold him until that point because he'd been so wired up. They let me hold him for the first time just before they gave us the news. That was the right way to do it; that I had that bonding time and was clinging onto him like mad.

They gave us some outdated leaflets with unflattering pictures of adults with Down's syndrome on. The prognosis wasn't great. Keith and I looked at each other. 'We're not going to listen to this; if he wants to do it he can, if he wants to do it, we won't put anything in his way.'

That determination, our determination, filtered into George because he is the most determined young man.

That's how George came to us.

A couple of years later, we were starting to think about a second baby. But we'd had two pregnancies that had ended in a shock of one sort or another. By then, we'd met lots of families with children of additional needs. We were aware of so many other things that could go wrong. It wasn't just the things that we knew about, there was so much that could go wrong. We weren't sure about having another one.

When George was 3½, we went on a weekend away organised by the National Deaf Children's Society for families with children with Down's syndrome who also had hearing loss. We sat on a table with a family who had three children, all of whom had Down's syndrome, all of whom had hearing loss, and all of whom were adopted.

We learnt so much that weekend about the support available for deaf children. What struck us most was this family that we'd met. Keith and I got in the car to come home and just looked at each other, 'Is there any chance you're thinking what I'm thinking?' Both believing that the other one was going to think we were off our rocker. Funnily enough we were both thinking the same thing.

A month later we met with an adoption agency, PACT [Parents and Children Together], and they accepted us as prospective adopters. We went through the adoption process and were approved in January the following year, seven months later. This was before the reforms – often others were taking more than a year to get through that first stage.

The process has since been massively streamlined. There are now time requirements on the agencies and the local authority. Stage one, for example, has to be completed within 8 weeks and stage two within 16 weeks.

From the perspective of the child who has had an unsteady start in life, and needs a new family, is there any check too rigorous to make sure that child is matched with the right family? It's so important that each child finds the right family. The social workers have to know a lot about you in order to make the right match.

CA: We were matched with Libby almost straight away. We went into the process knowing that we wanted to adopt a child with Down's syndrome. We wanted to use our experience and knowledge. We wanted George and his new sibling to have that sibling relationship that they could only have with another child with the same diagnosis.

CA: It can be a long wait for some people. There's a really difficult process that the adoption authorities ask you to go through – literally you have a piece of paper which is a long list of medical diagnoses. You have to tick whether you would or would not consider a child with x or y condition. With my role as an Adoption Champion, I'm really keen to help people demystify that form.

If you had asked me to complete that form five minutes before I'd given birth to George, would I have ticked 'Yes I'm happy to consider a child with Down's syndrome'? No, I wouldn't. When you look at it in black and white, it's very different to, 'Here's your much-longed-for baby and by the way he's got an extra chromosome and we'll need to teach you a few extra things along the way.'

CA: As an Adoption Champion I want to help prospective adopters not look on it as a black and white list of diagnoses. Instead, see the child behind; see the child who needs a family and ask themselves, 'Could I cope with this knowing that there's support out there; knowing that there are challenges ahead but enormous rewards too?'

SB: *I've noticed people use the term additional needs whereas in the past, people used the term special needs. Is there a difference between those terms? Does it upset parents to use the 'wrong' term?*

CA: You'd have to go a long way to upset me and I try not to shy away from an education opportunity. I would say to people, 'You've just used this word, and can I explain something to you about how that makes me feel?' All I ever ask is that you remember that they are children first. They are children who have Down's syndrome, not Down's children. That child bit comes first and George comes first. You can describe him as a child with a hearing loss as long as you've talked about him first because he is what's important.

As for additional needs vs special needs or children with disabilities: different people have different preferences. I tend to use 'additional needs' but I do use 'special needs' and I do use the term 'disabilities'. What is important is to ask people what term they prefer. I never mind explaining to people how I feel or what goes behind those thoughts. It's not about being politically correct; it's about you recognising that it's my child that's important.

I have many friends who have children on the autistic spectrum. Their challenges can come from the fact that the outside world perceives their child to be normal. To be the same as everybody else. When their behavioural challenges manifest out and about, you can get harsh judgement because other people don't realise what's going on.

SB: *They feel they're being judged on their parenting skills rather than the fact that their child has a sensory difficulty, for example.*

CA: Absolutely. Whereas I am never more grateful for the fact that my children wear their disability very visually than when George is sat in the middle of the road and refusing to move. People look and although the smiles I get might be a bit patronising, I very rarely feel personally criticised by it. I'm grateful for that.

George was 4½ when Libby came home and she was 12 months old. He loved having a little sister. In the early photos of the pair, they are just gazing at each other. In their most recent school photograph, they're sat next to each other and Libby's gazing up at him. That sums up their relationship. They're incredibly close. They seemed to know in those early days that they were going to learn a lot from each other. I'm so blessed to have these two children. My children aren't in pain, they don't suffer, they love life, they love their friends and everything they have the opportunity to do. They are both great gifts in my life.

SB: *Libby's an adopted child so you can't share her back-ground; was it a long process from when you were matched before she was allowed to come and live with you?*

CA: It was a long process in Libby's case through circum-stance rather than the process. Libby had open-heart surgery when she was nine months old which was around the time we were matched with her. Normally the process from matching to a child coming home is short; a couple of weeks. Libby needed surgery and it was felt to be in her best interests to stay with her foster carers with whom she had made that first attachment.

We had to wait for her to be strong enough and recovered from the surgery before it was appropriate to start introductions.

I wanted to explore with Carole whether there are more children in the adoption process with additional needs than without. Clumsily, I chose the wrong words and she took it as an opportunity to educate me... We made up for it after the interview.

SB: *Was Libby in the adoption process because of her additional needs?*

CA: This is where I give you an educational moment rather than telling you that you have said something wrong.

Libby's birth story and history is hers and very personal to her. You don't share it with everybody else. It isn't for me to share. When Libby's old enough to understand and choose how she wants other people to know or even if she wants other people to know, we'll let her share her story. Until then it's Libby's and not something that we discuss.

SB: *As an Adoption Champion, you support adoptive parents to manage those types of questions?*

CA: Yes, that is included in the preparation process. You go on a series of courses, preparation days and training days with other prospective adopters and experienced social workers.

If you adopt a much older child who has lived through much more of their own history, they may well be talking about it for themselves already. The training and preparation from your social worker is about helping your child find what they're comfortable talking about and what they don't want to talk about.

Libby was so young and her history is something that she doesn't understand in detail yet. It's really important to me that she has that opportunity to make that decision. It would feel like betraying a close confidence to share Libby's story with you. It saves you from making any unfair judgements.

Recently I was talking to a group of friends about George. One of them asked, 'Did you know he had Down's syndrome before you had him?' It's a really common question that people ask. But turn it on its head for a minute. That question is loaded with 'Would you have terminated your pregnancy?' People don't realise; often that isn't what they're asking, but the person they ask may feel that's the question they need to answer. It's an impossible question to answer when you have your baby in your arms. It can take a long time as a parent to find the confidence to say, 'Can I turn that question into a learning experience for you please?' instead of running away or crying.

The first time I cried from something somebody said to me, we were in special care. George was less than a month old. He had both his legs in plaster for his talipes. He had to have his casts changed every three or four days because he was growing so quickly.

Somebody in the waiting room asked me, 'Did you drop him, then?' I wished the ground would swallow me up. People don't always think; it's one of the harder bits about being a mum to children with additional needs. It can feel like you're constantly educating everybody else. It only takes one smile from one of those kids and it doesn't matter.

You rarely get upsetting questions from children. When Libby first started school I went into her class to read the storybook *My Friend Has Down's Syndrome* to her class. Afterwards, I asked, 'Do we know anybody who has Down's syndrome?' They all looked at me. 'The story book said that their face might be a particular shape and their eyes can be slightly almond shaped. It says they might find some things that we find easy, a bit more difficult to learn. Do you know anybody in our class who finds some things a bit more difficult?'

They were all staring at me as if I'd lost the plot. One little boy put his hand up and he said 'Round face and slightly different eyes? Father Christmas.' I beamed and beamed.

I replied 'I have no idea whether Father Christmas has Down's syndrome or not.' The children were all happy with that. When I asked, 'What about Libby? Do we think Libby might have Down's syndrome?' they said 'No, because Libby can do sign language and that's very clever.' I didn't have an answer to that, there wasn't one.

SB: *These education moments require a certain confidence. How do mums build that confidence?*

CA: It's the support that you have around you and it comes with time. When George was very young, I couldn't have done it. People gave me sound advice about not expecting too much of myself too soon.

These days I have an incredibly supportive network of friends.

To new mums, I'd say let other people learn with you. Don't try and learn it all on your own. Lots of the charity support organisations produce leaflets for other people.

The Down's Syndrome Association produce a publication for friends and family and a list of 'Do ask and Don't ask questions'.

The National Deaf Children's Society produce a fantastic leaflet for grandparents who can be daunted by the thought of learning to sign. Learn together and you will grow together.

I feel so lucky and blessed to be in the place that I'm in today. People like you Sherry who've come with me and who have had the opportunity to learn with me. When I first put a message on our antenatal group saying 'I've had my baby and goodness me it looks like he's got Down's syndrome,' you knew as much about it as I did. Yet none of you made me feel like I needed to be an expert straightaway.

I'm not an expert now, I'm still learning. We're about to start the transition into secondary school. I'm going back to the mums who supported me in the early months whose children are a couple of years older. Knocking on their door, 'Hello it's me again. There's a new challenge on the horizon and I need help to learn about this.'

Find out about local support groups ... and online support groups. There are organisations that match up families with children with specific diagnoses.

It's by sharing experiences that you gain confidence and the ability to talk about it.

SB: *When you talk to parents who don't have children with additional needs, does that complicate things or make it easier?*

CA: It goes through phases. In the early days I was able to accept support more readily from that online forum than from real people with real babies in real life. I struggled with those direct comparisons. You couldn't get away from the differences.

When I was talking to you online, I wasn't faced with the differences in such an obvious way. It's about finding the right support at the right time. As time went on, inclusion in mainstream groups became more important to me.

The adoption agencies and local authorities offer post-adoption support, whether or not you adopt a child with special needs.

We were unusual to adopt a child so young. 4% of adoptions last year were children under a year old. 76% were aged between one and four. Most children looking for forever families are in that older age bracket, not babies; they are toddlers and young children.

80% of all children in care are aged five and over. Older children are harder to place. When you're a prospective adopter, you're looking at things in a very black and white way and you're not picturing a child. You're picturing a baby. I help people to realise that adoptive children come in all sorts of shapes and sizes.

SB: *Part of your role as the Adoption Champion is to help prospective adoptive parents see that bigger picture and help them to understand the different options available to them.*

CA: I'm not making everything rosy by any stretch; it's not easy, but parenting isn't easy. Adopting a child with special needs isn't easy but the parenting rewards are enormous.

It was fascinating to talk to Carole and learn about the challenges and the rewards on her journey.

Key learning points

1. Get support.

2. Learn together and you will grow together.

3. Don't be afraid to share educational opportunities when somebody asks a clumsily worded question.

Additional resources

Adoption UK – the leading UK charity providing support, awareness and understanding for those parenting or supporting children who cannot live with their birth parents: www.adoptionuk.org/

Down's Syndrome Association – charity supporting people with Down's syndrome throughout their lives: www.downs-syndrome.org.uk/.

New Parents Pack: www.downs-syndrome.org.uk/download-package/new-parents-pack/.

National Deaf Children's Society – the leading charity dedicated to creating a world without barriers for deaf children and young people: www.ndcs.org.uk/.

PACT provides a summary and links to the stages of the adoption process: www.pactcharity.org/about-adoption.

For other mums, their experience of bringing up children is different and not what they expected because they become a single mum. This is the challenge that we explore in the next interview with Vivienne Smith.

The single mum's story

Vivienne Smith

Whether it's divorce, bereavement, separation – you can let it refine you but don't let it define you.

Vivienne Smith is a writer, trainer, presenter, transformational coach, and certified neurolinguistic programming (NLP) and hypnosis practitioner.

Her experience as a single mum prompted Vivienne to write a book about the subject. It has been the fulfilment of a long-term ambition to turn what was at the time a negative and distressing experience into an opportunity to help others get through similar challenges.

Now happily remarried, Vivienne provides support, practical advice and inspiration to single mothers everywhere through her book, coaching, seminars and webinars.

SB: *I've started working with a new client today who is at a crossroads. She is a single mum and wants to go back to work or set up her own business. Towards the end of our first session she said, 'I cannot believe that we've only been talking for 90 minutes and now I have all these ideas and thoughts. This is the first time in two years I have felt that I can start to be me again.' Is two years typical?*

VS: I remember someone telling me, 'It'll take you at least two years.' I thought, 'I don't want to spend two years of my life mourning.' It is like a bereavement. It's the death of your relationship. It's such an extreme position to be in and unless you've been there, it's difficult to imagine; it's that feeling of being alone. No-one is all alone and I really encourage single mums to ask for help. You want to be sure it's someone you trust, but do ask for help, because often people who care about you would love to help you and don't know how.

At first, what's difficult is that you're dealing with your own emotions. However you have to support your children with their emotions too. The saddest thing about a relationship break up is that children never would have chosen for their parents to be apart, and yet they have to process this incredible change. In our case, I had a very small baby (three weeks old) and a three year old. It was traumatic. We moved house and stayed with relatives. It was a period of extreme grief, shock, and trauma. Very quickly I had to learn how to put one foot in front of the other in order to care for my children.

As mothers, our overriding instinct is to look after the children. That gave me a focus, something to wake up for. You're doing the practical stuff but you are also dealing with their emotions.

Grief is a process. You have to go through the sadness, the hurt, maybe betrayal or possibly anger. You might get stuck in any one stage, however you have to allow yourself to go through those different processes. If you try and suppress it, it will come out later on. Suppressing emotions is not healthy. You have to learn how to give them expression, deal with them and move forward.

SB: *In your situation, not only were you dealing with the relationship bereavement but your three year old was coming to terms with a baby in the house. In my counsellor work, I see a lot of parents where a new baby is a big transition in itself.*

VS: You're all over the place. I went into total disbelief. It took me a while to adjust. It was heart-breaking; such a shock as I'd had no warning. We were about to move into our dream country cottage.

One of the things I'm proudest of is that I am still a trusting person. You have a choice: you can become bitter and twisted, and not trust anybody. You have to reassess everything you thought you knew about this other person and come to terms with the fact that you don't know them at all.

SB: *I imagine it makes you question yourself.*

VS: Absolutely, and so it should. I believe in seeing the opportunity in every situation. It forces you to take stock of everything. Why has this happened? You have to be aware that you may never come up with a decent answer.

You have a choice. When something happens to you, you have a choice whether to proceed as a victim or to decide that this is a sign that you're going to create a new life. Whether it's divorce, bereavement, separation – you can let it refine you but don't let it define you.

I think it's time to get to know yourself, to know what you love and don't love about how to bring up children, what your instincts are. You get a chance to be very mindful about your parenting, about what's important to you, in a way that you might not have done if you were still with your partner. That's not denigrating my children's father, because he's a very committed, hands-on dad and I can't criticise him in that respect at all.

However you do now have the opportunity to think, 'What is it I want to be as a mum? What's really important to me? What are the key things I want to teach my children as we go through this?'

If you are the primary carer, you are so influential in the way that your children form their opinions about families, love and relationships. You have a huge responsibility to conduct yourself in such a way that your children can heal with you and can come out of it with a positive, grounded approach to life. It doesn't have to scar them forever. It doesn't have to ruin everybody's life, not yours or your children's.

VS: To be frank, it's very hard to remove any conflict or bitterness from the situation in an acrimonious split. I made plenty of mistakes. But I've always said to the children, 'Your Dad loves you, we both love you.'

It's really important for them to understand that because they are a product of both of you. You don't want to make them feel bad about one parent because then they're feeling bad about themselves. Some time has passed since my first divorce and I'm able to be much more sanguine. Never stop the children from seeing their other parent, never stop them expressing positive things about the other parent.

VS: You don't want to censor your children. It's difficult not to use the children as pawns. It's really tempting to do that and pass bitter and twisted messages from one side to the other. Honestly, the kids have enough to deal with, without you putting your bitterness onto them.

You might not always do this brilliantly. What's really important is the children. The arguments and disagreements about money and access all fall away. As the grown ups, we can get help, coaching, or counselling in order to heal and come to terms with it. It's much tougher for the kids because they're not as sophisticated.

When I split from my second husband they were much older, however our lives remained pretty much the same. We had strong family values and there was minimal disruption when he eventually left because we had that solid grounding.

It wasn't an easy decision to make, but I knew I had to do it. For our own health and safety we needed to be away from him. If you give children that grounding, they can talk to you. You need to be able to talk honestly to them about their fears and issues. It's got to be age appropriate.

You can't brush it all under the carpet and pretend it's not happening because they'll make up stuff. Children will often feel responsible for everything. You don't want them to be thinking, 'If I'd been better,' or, 'Was it because I wasn't good enough last week?' or, 'I was naughty and is this punishment? Is it my fault?'

Keep drumming in, 'It's not your fault, we both love you.' Even if the parents aren't communicating very well, if my eldest was missing his dad, a phone call to his dad did wonders. Sometimes kids worry about stuff you haven't even considered, 'Where's Daddy living now? Who's cooking his meals? Is he doing the same job? What does he do at weekends?' You might not care, to be frank.

SB: *He's still their father, and if they have a good relationship with their father, they will care.*

VS: However upset they are or you are, it's useful to keep reminding them when they're next going to see Daddy or next going to speak to him. Sometimes for small children, you don't want to try and make them see the big picture. Little steps at a time. They can last for a few days knowing that Daddy's going to take them to football as normal.

I'm assuming your ex or the absent parent is willing and able, and prepared to play along. One of the challenges is how to co-parent peacefully. Often the conflict and the bitterness will spill over and continue for many years. It's encouraging people and giving them the tools to build a good working relationship. I know that sounds cold, but sometimes that's the easiest way to think of it, so that when you discuss the children, you remove as much of the emotion as you can.

Try to keep to the point and work out what's the best thing for the children when you're discussing arrangements. You don't need to load that conversation with emotion – anger or sadness – because it's not helpful. Tempting, but not helpful.

SB: *You talked about the grief cycle earlier. If you get stuck in one of those stages, it must be difficult to do as you're suggesting.*

VS: And that's why I say be sure to get help, because no one's superwoman. You're going to find this tough. You didn't sign up for this. I thought I would be married for life and everything was going to be rosy and wonderful.

And don't worry about occasionally losing it. You're human. On the whole, people are willing to help. There is so much support and sympathy out there. Don't worry about being perfect and don't be too proud to occasionally have a wobbly moment. They'll hit you when you're least expecting it. I always put tissues in my bag to go to school plays. I would catch myself looking round thinking, 'Everybody else is happy and here's me...'

SB: *You don't know what's behind those other faces...*

VS: Chances are that half the audience are not in a happy family. You tend to assume that you're the only one in pain, but you're not.

Do tell the school what's going on. They will be used to it and they can look out for any behaviour that your child's exhibiting and understand it for what it is. The last thing you want is for your child to be told off because they're misbehaving when they're having a rotten time and acting out what they're going through. Tell the school and they'll be extra understanding and keep an eye on your child.

The legal side can be terrifying for some people. You have to deal with the legal things. Be prepared. Get as much information together as you can and you'll feel relieved once you've got it underway. The worst thing is to put your head in the sand and go into denial. There are lots of things you can do to help reduce your costs. These days there are wonderful things like collaborative law and mediators. You don't necessarily have to go through the adversarial court appearance that people imagine. You don't want the lawyers to be making more money out of your misery than necessary. Get empowered, get prepared. Face up to things but know that you're not by yourself.

Finances can be terrifying; in many relationships it's the man who deals with the finances. There are lots of free resources and there might be benefits that you're entitled to. Knowing what you're facing is more empowering than worrying about it because you're too scared to check.

SB: *Get started on dealing with that legal stuff, because as scary as it might sound, it's better to know what you're dealing with than worry about what you don't know.*

VS: The worst is fear of the unknown. If you feel scared doing this by yourself, find a friend or relative who's happy to be your accountability buddy.

Asking for help is the thing that people do last and should do first. People do want to help you. Not everyone, but the people who really care about you will want to help you. It could be something very simple that would mean a lot to you.

When people feel depressed or down, it can have the knock-on effect of making them feel very tired.

It is important to look after yourself and that includes getting some exercise, and getting sleep. I was staying up all night because I didn't get any time to myself during the day, but that doesn't work for too long, because you will run on empty after a while.

Look for ways that you can conserve your energy and get 'me' time as well. Some mums might say, 'My ex disappeared off into wherever and I never see him so he never has the children.'

But for most relationships, you do have time when the children are with their other parent. I encourage you to have a plan to make the most of that time, because it can go really quickly.

Plan at least one fun thing. You can spend time catching up with the chores, however what's really important is to do something wonderful just for you.

It could be catching up with a friend, going to a gallery, watching a film, having a duvet day with a box of chocolates and your favourite movie. Something that will lift your spirits.

Look after yourself, because you're the most important person to your children. You've got to keep yourself strong and feeling resourceful so you can cope. You'll be a much better mum when you've had time to recharge and recoup.

SB: *One of my clients wanted to start a beginners' running course on Saturday mornings while her ex-husband looked after the children. However she found that she couldn't rely on him.*

VS: If your ex is being unreliable, this may be a phase. It may be that he will improve and things will settle down, so don't despair. If he is unreliable, don't make him the person you rely on when it's something really important. Make your standby your mum or your best friend. Maybe you could do childcare swaps with a friend.

It makes you feel much better if you're not beholden to somebody. I've got good at accepting help with good grace, but it can be difficult to swallow your pride.

SB: *What if your ex doesn't turn up or phone the children at the expected time, how do you manage this so that the children don't get too upset?*

VS: One of the mums I spoke to, her ex was so unreliable she continued to encourage her son to be open to the possibility that his father was going to turn up but they had a lot of disappointments and times when he didn't manage it. When her son got to age 12, he made the decision that he didn't want to see his father for a bit. She supported him because she felt that it was doing him more harm than good.

He has since developed a relationship with his Dad who is trying very hard to make up for lost time. Listen to your intuition, your gut feeling and think about it from your child's point of view.

Don't have a furious phone call with your ex while your child is listening. Instead say, 'I'm going to contact Daddy later to see what happened. Maybe his car broke down or maybe he got held up. I know that he's really keen to see you and I'll make sure we can talk to him on the phone later on, even if he isn't able to come today, but I understand that you're feeling sad and angry.'

Never make them do the stiff upper lip thing. Children will get angry and sad. You probably will bear the brunt of it because that's your job as the mum. It's really important to make it ok for your child to be embarrassed, upset, disappointed, angry, and say, 'That's alright, I understand.' *Dinosaurs Divorce* by Laurene Krasny Brown is a good tool to talk to your child about his or her feelings.

Find a safe way for them to talk about how they feel. Sometimes children will do that through role play with toys. 'Why is elephant looking so sad today? What's happened?' You might find your child finds it easier to talk as if it's not about them. For others, it might be drawing a picture.

It will get messy. There's no way of avoiding that. As long as they feel they can come to you and feel safe to discuss it, you're doing a good job. You can't control everybody else's behaviour: what you can do is be the safe space and that'll count for a lot. You don't need to make up excuses if you don't want to. Don't lie about anything that's happening, but you don't need to make things worse.

It's about accepting and acknowledging the feelings that your children are experiencing without brushing them aside. You're the mum. You're the expert on your child. Give yourself space to listen to your intuition and you will find the best way to deal with it.

SB: *What about forgiveness? That's a tough one to deal with.*

VS: Forgiveness is the chapter that took me the longest to write because I clearly had some forgiveness work to do for myself. Forgiveness is very important.

I struggled with forgiveness because I didn't want to condone what had happened. I understood that unless I was able to accept and come to some sort of resolution, I couldn't move forward because I'd be continually dragging this burden along with me.

You are going to be the person most bothered by the fact that you can't forgive someone. The anger and the bitterness will eat you up from inside. You may know people who haven't forgiven and you can see how corrosive that is.

One of the biggest challenges is learning how to forgive. You need to come to terms with what's happened, how you've behaved, how they've behaved. You may not be able to change what's happened but you can change how you remember that.

You need to find a way forward so that you can be civil and professional in the way that you deal with things. You can't go off to separate corners of the world and never speak to each other again. That's not real life. You will always be in a relationship, because you will always have these children.

The other person may not be playing ball and may not be conducting themselves fairly and honourably. However you will have the satisfaction of knowing that you've conducted yourself with dignity. Your children will see that. It will be noticed and it will have a positive effect. In the end it will have a positive effective on the other person. If you keep behaving in a reasonable and fair way, what are they going to do?

Be aware that you may not feel in control but you have a lot of control over the way things turn out. You can make them turn out well by being the best person you can be, the person who considers: do I love my kids more than I hate my ex?

SB: *When you've been through a divorce, those feelings are so powerful and strong.*

VS: Absolutely, and I wouldn't minimise any of that. If you feel that it's taking over, please get help. Your friends and family are not trained to help you to deal with that and it's not fair to burden them with it. They will have their own opinion about why things have gone wrong; what you should have done and what he should have done. Sometimes it's not helpful for you.

The key is to find impartial, preferably professional help, someone who is used to leading you through the minefields and getting you safely to the other side. You want to move forward into a new life, whether as a contentedly single person or with a new partner.

SB: *I haven't been through a divorce myself but there have been divorces in my family. My parents' marriage broke up when I was 12 or 13 so I can empathise with the feelings of the children. I know the hurt and pain and it's not just immediate family – father, mother, child – it's the grandparents, the sisters and brothers.*

VS: It affects everybody and that's one of the saddest things. Being aware that it has a wider impact can often help people to conduct themselves in an honourable way.

Let the children continue to have contact with the grandparents wherever possible, as long as it's safe and good for them. You might struggle to have good relationships with his family but your children need them because they're part of their family as well. Remember you're doing it for the kids.

SB: *As you said earlier, you're modelling the behaviour and emotional resilience that you want your children to develop.*

VS: You don't want these cycles of behaviour to go through the generations. You can stop that cycle at any time and I encourage people to be the one that changes for the positive.

You don't want your children growing up thinking divorce is inevitable because it's not.

SB: *From a teenager's perspective, my parents' marriage break up wasn't pleasant. I hardly ever heard my dad say a bad word about my mother and similarly with my mum. Mostly they were civil towards each other. It affected me when I had my first long-term boyfriend. I didn't want to commit because I didn't want a marriage break up. Having said that, I've been happily married for 27 years now.*

VS: I think it's safe to say that it's worked! It made you more cautious maybe and that's not such a bad thing. If I could teach my kids anything it would be, listen to your instincts.

Key learning points

1. Ask for help; people are willing to help but often don't know what help to offer.

2. You have a choice: remain bitter and twisted or accept what's happened and learn from it.

3. Don't delay dealing with the legal or financial aspects: just get started. It's better to know what you're facing than worry about the unknown.

4. Plan your time when your children are with your ex and include at least one fun thing.

5. Learn to forgive: anger and bitterness are corrosive.

6. Provide a safe way for your children to explore their feelings.

7. Be honourable, civil and professional, for the sake of your children.

Additional resources

Gingerbread – charity providing expert advice and practical support for single parents: www.gingerbread.org.uk/

SingleParents.org.uk – run by Single Parent Action Network, this site brings together essential information, expert advice, interactive learning, multi-media content, links to other support organisations and news for anyone who is parenting alone: www.singleparents.org.uk

The Confident Mother looks after herself and her family by eating healthily, active movement throughout the day, dressing the part and sounding the part. Discover how to boost your confidence with these next four interviews packed full of practical advice.

Confidence in what you feed your family: fats, sugar and supplements

Lucy Grainge

Fats are fabulous!

Lucy Grainge is The Food Owl, a nutritional therapist and mum to two. Food runs in the family – her mum was a trained chef. When she left university, she started a career in banking working long hours and it was there that her diet went downhill; she noticed that she struggled with energy levels and would need sugar and caffeine pick-me-ups in the afternoon. When she began experiencing uncomfortable gut problems she consulted a nutritional therapist, who suspected a candida overgrowth and blood sugar imbalance. Lucy worked with the therapist, taking supplements and following a healthier diet, and gradually, over time, her energy was restored and the gut symptoms subsided. These experiences led Lucy to retrain as a nutritional therapist, as she saw this would also provide a more flexible career than the bank.

LG: It's one thing being responsible for your own nutrition, it's another being responsible for your children's and even your partner's. I will try to be practical and pragmatic. You have heard conflicting advice and I'll attempt to pick through that so that you have some really clear messages. Let's start with fats, good fats vs bad fats.

I always encourage my clients to eat more fat. You might think I'm bonkers but it comes up more and more in the press. As a society, we are fat deficient. We're deficient in the good fats, the healthy fats that we need for our brains to function properly, for our children's brains to grow properly. We need fats for energy, warmth, growth hormone production, healthy skin and hair.

Your skin should be supple and a bit shiny. Most of us walk round with dry, flaky skin and pile the moisturiser on every day. If your diet is sufficient in healthy fats, you don't need to do that. We didn't evolve to have this integral need for the potions and lotions that we slap on ourselves.

We need fat to help the body absorb the fat-soluble vitamins: A, D, E and K. Lower IQ, attention deficit disorder, allergies, eczema, depression, fatigue, and cardiovascular disease are all associated with deficiencies of essential fats. There are so many reasons to eat healthy fats like nuts, seeds and oily fish, such as sardines, mackerel, or salmon. Eat fish or take a fish oil supplement. There is a wealth of scientific evidence that these fats are healthy for us, preventing cardiovascular disease, diabetes, and more.

White fish such as cod or plaice are good to eat too, however you do not get your essential fats from those fish.

The other good fats are in nuts and seeds. With younger children, it's difficult to offer nuts because of the choking hazard. As for the allergy issue – bear in mind that peanuts are a legume not a nut. Tree nuts such as almonds, walnuts, cashews etc. are from a different family. If you have a history of peanut allergy in the family, it's unlikely that there will be a tree nut allergy unless that's already been identified.

Other fats that I want you to include are the monounsaturated fats that we get from olive oil and avocados. Avocado is lovely for weaning because it's nice and soft, and you can include it in purees.

The fats to avoid are the vegetable fats that become damaged when they're manufactured. Sunflower seed and vegetable oils in plastic bottles are polyunsaturated fats. We know now that these damage our arteries and lead to heart disease. Cooking with those fats is even more problematic because it produces *trans fats*.

Avoid hydrogenated fats too. They are less common in our food today. The hydrogenation process was invented at the turn of the last century to produce cheap fats to help feed armies in Europe. It was during the Second World War that it came into its own in the UK. Butter was an expensive fat because dairy farming had been reduced and we had rationing. Food manufacturers were trying to meet demand. Scientists created a process turning cheap vegetable oils into spreads and margarine. Hydrogenation is the process whereby they insert the hydrogen atom into the oil chemically which makes the oil hard. It turns into this grey, sludgy hard mass. They add yellow food colouring and hey presto, margarine.

The hydrogenating process enabled us to have cheap, spreadable fats. Today we know that hydrogenated fats are directly linked to heart disease. Hydrogenated fats are still found in lower-quality biscuits, cakes and confectionery, as well as cosmetics – look at the label for 'hydrogenated' or 'partially hydrogenated' fat/oil.

SB: *If we avoid hydrogenated fats, and sunflower or vegetable oil are damaged fats, what is left to cook with?*

LG: It's ok to cook with butter or ghee (clarified butter). Butter is an unprocessed food product. It's churned milk and it contains vitamins. I love butter. I'm not saying eat tons of it but I'd rather you ate that than a processed 'butter' spread.

You can cook with light olive oil which is a refined olive oil. Don't cook with extra virgin olive oil at high temperature. It's very delicate. It's been extracted on a cold press without heat. Normally you buy it in a dark glass bottle. Use it cold, on your salad dressings, in a bit of mayonnaise maybe with another cold expressed oil. Use it drizzled on your hot vegetables but don't cook with it at high temperatures. It damages the oil, it will damage you and it's a waste of a beautiful oil.

SB: *What about animal fats – chefs rave about duck fat and goose fat.*

LG: Yes, those fats are stable at high temperatures and give a nice flavour to your potatoes and parsnips. They're not going to damage you because they don't become damaged at high temperatures, unlike vegetable oils.

When you buy oils, look at the packaging. Avoid buying oils in plastic bottles. Plastics are lipophilic which means they dissolve into the fat or oil. The bottles leach plastic particles into the oil which then go into you.

One that's become popular as a superfood is coconut oil. I love coconut oil; it does have a slight coconut flavour, but it is possible to buy deodorised coconut oil if you really hate the faint taste. If you're vegetarian or you can't face the thought of using a traditional animal fat to roast or fry, try coconut oil. You can buy it in most supermarkets. It's solid at room temperature. You don't need much. It's a good appetite suppressor (a teaspoon or so) but in a healthy way. Some people spread it on toast.

Moving on to sugars

LG: Let's start with fruit juice – if you have fruit juice, always dilute it at least 50/50. I did introduce fruit juice early to my daughter simply because I couldn't get her to drink anything. She wouldn't drink water, she hated milk after the age of two, and she was getting urinary tract infections. I was pretty desperate. The advice is don't give them anything other than milk and water but sometimes Sherry, even as the nutritionist, you do whatever you can to get some hydration into your child.

It wasn't ideal because I was introducing another source of sugar into her diet that was perhaps unnecessary but it was a means to an end. If it's part of a meal that will help, because that will mitigate the impact of those sugars on your child's bloodstream.

You want to avoid sugars on your teeth, too. On our table at home we always have a packet of straws. Anything with sugars, even milk (lactose in milk is a type of sugar), is drunk through a straw to have less impact on the teeth. I buy a pack of 200 different colour straws. Useful if you're out in a café. They can drink through a straw and although it's the same amount of sugar, at least their teeth aren't attacked as badly.

Smoothies have got a lot of bad flak recently. Some shop-bought smoothies might have six and half teaspoons of sugar in a 250ml bottle. The advantage of smoothies is that it's the whole fruit, particularly if you make them yourself. You get the fibre as well as the other nutrients. Part of the confusion with fruit is that when we look at studies, people who include fruit as part of their diet tend to have lower risk of heart disease, diabetes, and other chronic diseases. However people who include fruit juice in their diet, don't.

We're discovering that it's about the other nutrients in the fruit and the fibre. The body can cope with fruit sugars in reasonable amounts, two or three pieces of fruit a day. It's about the whole package. It's preferable to have a home-made smoothie to a fruit juice. Get yourself a powerful blender if you want more fruit in your diet in a healthier way. The ideal is to eat the fruit as it is, but it's not the end of the world to have a smoothie, preferably with a meal or with a snack that involves protein and fat to slow down digestion.

If you're using squash it's better to have a sugar squash than to have sugar-free squash. Sugar-free squashes contain artificial sweeteners, such as acesulfame K, aspartame, and saccharin. Artificial sweeteners are toxic. In animal studies they're carcinogenic, though in studies they're using thousands of times the actual dosage that you get in a glass of squash. However I have concerns about loading over a lifetime. Some brands of squash and fizzy drinks are now using a natural sweetener called stevia – you might see it listed as 'steviol glycosides' on the ingredients list. This is derived from a plant and is considered safe.

Artificial sweeteners are not just in squash they're in diet foods such as yogurts. We all thought that sugar free was much better. However it is confusing for the body to have sweeteners. If you're having sugar or fructose in high amounts, it's not fantastic but the body can recognise those sugars and knows what to do with them. The body has hormones to process them.

Sweeteners are confusing because you give signals to the brain, 'I've eaten sugar,' when you haven't.

That kicks off an insulin response, because the body is expecting sugar. When you don't get the sugar, it can make you hungry and crave more sweet things.

The body says, 'Hang on, where is it then? I've just kicked out a lot of insulin.' That pushes your blood sugar too low and that will make you feel a bit weak, dizzy or irritable.

You get yourself onto a rollercoaster. That's what happened to me when I was working for the bank. My diet was poor. I was relying on Diet Coke because I thought it was better than the fat Coke. I was relying on caffeine to boost my adrenal levels so that I felt better because I'd pushed my blood sugar levels too low. Then I was grabbing chocolate. It is easy to get into this spiral and it can happen with your children as well. Your body doesn't know what to do with sweeteners and stores them as toxins in your fat.

Stay away from sweeteners; sugar is not great but it's better than artificial sweeteners. There are healthier sweeteners on the market now, such as stevia or polyols. Anything ending in -ol will be a polyol such as sorbitol or maltitol. It's a kind of a sugar alcohol which won't impact on your blood sugar. Be careful of the amounts, particularly with children, as they can cause temporary loose stools.

I often get asked about Agave syrup – it's mainly fructose so it doesn't affect your blood sugar balance because fructose is processed by the liver. However too much fructose is a problem because your liver will turn it to fat and too much leads to Non-alcoholic Fatty Liver disease.

The fatty liver causes diabetes because it stops the pancreas from working properly. It stops the cells producing the insulin and the glucagon that's needed to regulate blood sugar.

After covering fats and sugars, we moved on to food supplements.

LG: I often get asked, do I need to supplement? Is it a waste of money? Am I just going to have expensive urine?

In my opinion and from my research, it's very difficult to have the optimum level of nutrients in your diet and in your child's diet. We can achieve the daily recommended allowance. However the confusion is that people believe that the recommended daily allowance is something to aim for. RDAs are to stop people becoming deficient, to prevent diseases such as rickets, scurvy, beriberi. RDAs are the minimum.

Most people's diets are not perfect. I know my children's diets are far from perfect because their eating is erratic. If you lead a hectic lifestyle, juggling work, children, and looking after parents, you may be running yourself ragged. You may not have the time to make nutritious homemade meals every day. You could do worse than take a good multivitamin and mineral. Don't feel it's a failure; I would say that it's a necessity.

Our fruit and vegetables don't contain the same level of vitamins and minerals that they used to. Over the past 60 years, data on mineral and nutrient levels has been recorded, and levels have dropped because of intensive farming practices.

The government guidelines say that children between six months and five years should have daily supplements of vitamins A, C and D, most parents I speak to are not even aware it's a standard government recommendation

SB: *And today of course, food is transported long distances and can lose some of its nutritional value during transportation and the refrigeration process?*

LG: We are so much better at storing food at cold temperatures in warehouses which means food can be sitting around for days, weeks, months even. Oranges might have been in storage for ages and lose their vitamin C content quite rapidly. It looks like an orange but may have one tenth of the vitamin C content it had when it was on the tree.

SB: *A vitamin and mineral supplement helps to compensate for the modern lifestyle.*

LG: Absolutely, even a basic supplement. Vitamin D is key. Between September and April it's not physically possible to get enough vitamin D from the sun in the UK. You can stand there all day in the winter sunshine and you will not make any vitamin D in your skin. The sunlight is not at the right angle.

I would like to mention fish oils – fish doesn't always go down well with children. There are nice tasting fish oil supplements; some are mixed with fruit concentrates. You're only having a teaspoon or two so you don't need to worry about the fruit sugars.

There are chewable ones too. There is so much evidence about the impact on the brain, our IQ levels and behaviour. Vegetarians can use flax seed oil.

Finally, probiotics...

LG: Probiotics are the little bugs, the bacteria that we hear about, which keep the gut healthy. 70% of your immune system is in your gut. If your gut isn't working properly, your gut lining isn't healthy and you're going to have immune problems. These normally start manifesting themselves as food intolerances or allergies.

It's believed that we see more food allergies because we have too many antibiotics. Antibiotics save lives and are fantastic in acute situations. They kill the bug that is making you ill and that is the outcome you want. The side effect is that antibiotics will decimate the probiotic bugs that line your intestine. This leaves space for pathogenic bacteria to take hold of the gut.

People might find that they start having more tummy upsets after a couple of rounds of antibiotics. Or you might become more constipated than before. If your doctor has ruled out anything more serious, think back to whether you have had a course of antibiotics recently? I recommend that you take 30 days of probiotics after every course of antibiotics. You can get them as chewable tablets in most chemists now. My take away is that any time you or your child has antibiotics, supplement for a month afterwards with probiotics.

LG: Fats are fabulous, just think about that.

Key learning points

1. Fats are fabulous; most of us don't eat enough fats.

2. There are good fats and bad fats. Yes to monoun-saturated fats and essential fats found in oily fish, nuts, seeds, olives, avocados: no to hydrogenated fats and oils in plastic bottles.

3. Sugars – water down fruit juice and drink through a straw.

4. Avoid artificial sweeteners e.g. acesulfame K, aspar-tame, saccharin.

5. Include a vitamin and mineral supplement; especial-ly Vitamin D and fish oil.

6. Use probiotics after a course of antibiotics.

Discover how to boost your confidence through the way you speak in the next interview with Susan Heaton Wright.

Project confidence through your voice and presence

Susan Heaton Wright

That's neat, that's neat, I really love your diva feet!

Susan Heaton Wright is a former opera singer and mum to a teenage boy. She runs two businesses: Viva Live Music organises live entertainment mainly for corporate events, and Executive Voice trains people to use their voice, their performance and their physical presence effectively when public speaking, whether that is webinars, presentations, meetings, or on the telephone. When she was at school, Susan was very shy and wouldn't say boo to a goose; now she teaches others to use their voice to project confidence. In this interview she shares her tips on how to do this.

SHW: The voice and our body language are closely connected. If I lack confidence, my shoulders might go up, my head might be down and it alters my voice. It creates tension around the neck area and the shoulders. The air goes through our larynx (or voice box) to create our voices and is compressed when we are tense.

I always think about my feet; if your feet are firmly on the ground, I call it diva feet (or divo feet for men). Make sure that your feet are grounded and your knees are soft. Try to make sure that your shoulders are relaxed and your head's up; not star gazing but in front, not looking down.

It's a neutral position: not threatening, not weak, not aggressive. It is neutral and friendly. Vocally it makes your voice sound better. If you wear heels, practise in front of the mirror in your high heels.

People might buy a new pair of shoes for an important presentation. However they then sometimes look awkward because it's a slightly different heel height than they might be used to. There's nothing wrong with a smart pair of shoes, your much loved ones that you know you're not going to trip over.

If you are sat around a table at a business meeting, call on your Sitting Diva. Sit down on your chair with feet firmly on the ground, your knees at 90 degrees and your hips at 90 degrees. Sit on your sitting bones. From there relax the shoulders so that you can breathe easily from the abdominal muscles.

Petite ladies can find it slightly intimidating in meeting situations. Try what Sheryl Sandberg says, lean in. Sit on the edge of your chair, making sure you don't fall off, put your elbows on the table and lean slightly in. Make sure you can still breathe, and that you're relaxed at the shoulders. This gives you more physical presence. As kids we are told no elbows at the dinner table. This is different – it's with your forearms flatter. Don't put one hand in front of another because that's creating a barrier.

Be aware of what you're doing in meetings. Do you huddle up? Cross your arms? Cross your legs? Are you like a dormouse in a hibernation ball? It creates a barrier and affects your voice.

SB: *A challenge for me personally is that I have a naturally quiet voice. I'm not nervous about public speaking. How do I make my voice louder without shouting?*

SHW: Think about a guitar which has six strings. If you pluck a string, the sound isn't loud. The sound is made by the sound waves going into the sound box, the wooden part of the guitar. We hear the wood resonating and vibrating. With our voice, we want to use what we can to resonate the sound to project those sound waves. Our bones do this.

Men have lower voices and naturally use the bones in their chest more. For ladies, we have to get the sound into our heads. When you speak, think about your voice going into your facial mask; coming out of your eyes, your nose and your mouth, not your throat.

Make sure that your neck and shoulders are relaxed and that you're not pushing the voice, because then the shoulders and neck tense. Relax and think about the voice coming from your face.

SB: *The female voice tends to be higher than the male voice. For some of us, our voices tend to rise when we're nervous. What tips do you have for calming yourself down?*

SHW: Everybody's voice goes higher when they're frightened or stressed. Women's voices are naturally higher pitched so it's more noticeable. Margaret Thatcher famously altered hers; she had vocal training to lower her voice.

I have a routine before a presentation or public speaking engagement. One of the things that can happen is that your mouth can go dry. I make sure that I remain hydrated throughout the day. It makes a huge difference from a physical point of view. Get there early and check the room for anything technical such as PowerPoint and the microphone. I have a warm-up routine and do some hula-hoop exercises, that hip action, to relax and energise me.

I use series of exercises to relax the neck, jaw, face, arms, legs, and hips. I do power breathing. You take a deep breath and you breathe in, 'I am confident.' Your body will adopt that confident persona. Practise at home.

If you have a tendency to speak fast when nervous, try and pause and take a couple of deep breaths to slow down the heartbeat. When you breathe fast, the shoulders go up because you're shallow breathing. Consciously think of taking a deep breath and taking your time to consciously slow down to relax yourself. And think of your feet.

If you blush when nervous, develop a routine for relaxing as much as possible. The power breath without hyperventilating; think 'I am confident' to internalise the emotion of being confident. Think very positive thoughts before you go on.

With speaking, if you're expected to do presentations or public speaking for work with little experience, that can be tough. Gain confidence and build it up. Get experience, maybe chairing local NCT or PTA meetings. Make sure that you talk at these committee meetings to give you the confidence to do it at another level.

If you have a strong accent, and you are aware that your audience might not be able to understand what you say, speak more slowly and pay particular attention to your diction. Make it as easy as possible for your audience to understand you

Final tips: be brave, because if you speak up, that gives you confidence. Be firm, be heard, keep the voice low-pitched.

SB: *For me, I have learned that I need to talk through my face, think about diva feet and sitting diva, get experience in my local community.*

Key learning points

1. Remember your diva feet, well grounded.

2. Sitting diva at meeting tables.

3. Lean in at meetings.

4. Talk through your face.

5. Develop a relaxing routine to calm your nerves.

6. Get experience in your community.

In the next interview with Vicky Warr, we discover how to boost body confidence through fitness.

Get fit to get confident

Vicky Warr

Exercise shouldn't be considered a chore, it should be something that you enjoy because it makes you feel good.

Vicky Warr, Founder of the Beez Kneez and Beez Kneez Hive, is a pregnancy and postnatal fitness expert. Previously Vicky had worked in the corporate world in an advertising agency, working long hours and not getting much exercise. When she started going to weekly fitness classes, she loved the benefits it gave her: more energy, more focus, more clarity, plus she was in better physical shape. She went on to train as an aerobics instructor, then as a personal trainer before taking an additional qualification in pregnancy and postnatal fitness. For the past nine years, Vicky has specialised in working with mums and mums-to-be. Vicky explains what that means.

VW: A postnatal fitness specialist is somebody who has trained specifically in postnatal exercise prescription; who has studied anatomy and what happens when you have a baby; who knows about abdominal separation, has worked with physiotherapists and perhaps has had children themselves; who understands situations such as twins and how different birth experiences can affect your body and your muscles, both internally and externally. It's important to seek out somebody who has the experience and the knowledge. Up to 12 months is still postnatal, and after that it is beyond the natal.

However if you have had children, your body has changed and your hormones have changed. For mums of teenagers, it could be that issues such as abdominal separation were not addressed when they had the babies, and issues can appear much further down the line, for example pelvic floor or incontinence issues.

Exercise is not a priority for many people, when we've done all the other things that we have to do as a working mum. However exercise makes you feel good and it helps you sleep better. It gives you mental clarity, improves your health and your heart. The health benefits are huge. The pros far outweigh the cons. Exercise shouldn't be considered a chore, it should be something that you enjoy because it makes you feel good.

I haven't always been into fitness but when I discovered how good it made me feel, how my stress levels reduced, it was something that I made a priority because it made me feel so much better.

Not having enough time is the reason many people give for not doing any exercise. However you just need to find ten minutes here and there when you can do some movement. Something that you enjoy or strength exercises or abdominal exercises and a quick video in ten minutes. Exercise doesn't have to take hours out of your day. Little and often is the best way.

SB: *As Julia Harris said in her interview, it's not time man-agement; it's the self-management concept. Treating yourself as important and valuing yourself. We know that your self-esteem feeds into the self-esteem of your children.*

VW: Exactly. Looking after yourself means you can look after other people. Ten minutes is all you need and a ten-minute specialist video at home is the perfect solution. That's why I created the Beez Kneez Hive, to help mums who don't have enough time to do fitness.

Doing it at home doesn't require travelling time. You don't need lots of equipment. If you multi-task your muscles, using your own bodyweight and resistance bands, you get a very effective workout.

SB: *Before I bought weights to use at home, I used tins of baked beans or some of the children's toys to give me extra resistance. It doesn't need to cost a lot of money.*

VW: Exactly. You can do some great exercises in the kitch-en while you're waiting for the kettle to boil. One of the best exercises is the **squat** because it strength-ens your hips, your thighs and your glutes. The glu-tes is one area that really weakens during pregnancy and a weak muscle is an untrained muscle. Getting a squat correct is a case of strengthening and open-ing out your hips. People often have very tight hips due to sitting for the majority of their day. If you do two minutes of squats while you're waiting for the kettle to boil, you have a great leg and a great bottom workout.

Squats strengthen the glutes which are part of the core. The core is not just about your tummy muscles. Your core is the whole of your torso from the chest down to the bottom of the glutes, so strengthening that whole area is really important.

SB: *I found that it helps to find a time of day to hang it on. I try and do core work when I first get up before the children are awake before breakfast. Pinning it to another part of my routine helps.*

VW: It's great to schedule your 10- to 15-minute slots into your diary for the week, allowing for flexibility in case things crop up. Put them in as an appointment because accountability is key.

If you've got somebody to hook up with as well, someone who is keeping you accountable, you can have great fitness success. Does your gym ever email you to say, 'We noticed you haven't been in this week?' Not often. That's why personal trainers are popular, because you have the accountability.

It depends on what you want to get from your fitness. However if you want to get into shape, ten minutes once a week isn't going to hit it.

Look at your stress factors because that can affect your ability to get into shape, particularly around your tummy. Eat good quality, protein-based meals that are fresh and unprocessed. Move around in the day.

People forget about movement. They sit down all day at a desk, then go out and exercise for an hour. But we're not moving naturally during our day.

Moving around the office or around your home office, stretching for a couple of minutes, rotating your neck, moving your arms, circulating your arms, stretching is great. When you're sat down, your muscles get very short, very tight and they're not at their optimal length. You need to be moving or taking a 20-minute power walk to clear your head, outside ideally. Walking is one of the best natural movements. If you're sat down during your day job, you want to be getting up and being upright so that you're using your core muscles and your core muscles are learning to support your spine. They can only do that in the upright position.

If you enjoy swimming, that's great. It's very low impact and you don't have to swim up and down, you can walk through the water. It's great for your pelvic floor if you have issues after you've had a baby.

It won't necessarily tone you up and strengthen your core unless you're doing a combination of strokes and breast stroke. If you're going to go swimming you do need to mix it up, use a variety of strokes but also ensure you're doing strength training as well so using your body or weights and doing exercises that require multiple muscles.

What happens when you're seated: we tend to round our shoulders. The shoulders come forward and the chest muscles become very tight. We tend to jut our heads forwards and the chin comes forward like a turkey. That places stress around the upper back and neck. When you're sat down the core muscles aren't used at all which can lead to back ache and stiff, niggly feelings in your lower back.

Your hips are at a permanent 90-degree angle and so are your knees, which means your hamstrings, at the back of your thighs, tighten up. Moving further down the legs, your calf muscles at the back of your lower leg: all these muscles get very tight.

Before I had babies, I loved my running and I did the London Marathon a couple of times. Running my own business, I face the same challenges that every mum out there faces in terms of fitting in fitness. For the days when I have so much on, I stretch for five or ten minutes twice a day and I'll walk for ten minutes.

It's a priority for me because I know how it makes me feel. I don't spend hours going to a gym. I don't have a gym membership. It didn't work for me. I could never get to the classes on time after having children.

I do four or five sessions of 15 to 20 minutes a week, but they are quality sessions. I keep it low impact, I move and I combine that with sleeping and good quality food. I'm a foodie so it is important to me to eat well.

I keep alcohol to moderation. Alcohol contains a lot of sugar which makes me hugely lethargic and I don't have mental clarity or focus. It disturbs my sleep which doesn't make me productive the next day. Having said that, I love champagne so on special occasions I will have a few glasses.

SB: *For mums with primary school children, we could add few minutes on the way back from the school run to make the walk a bit longer?*

VW: Yes and ideally, go a slightly hillier route and pick up the pace. Make sure you've got the right footwear. When you're walking, it's important that you walk correctly with the right gait: striking with your heel and then the ball of your foot; your legs are fairly straight and you're swinging your arms by your side. Then walking is very effective, you'll burn more calories and raise your metabolism.

When mums have just had babies, there's a huge emphasis on trying to get back into shape. One of the worst things that you can do is to start running and jogging on muscles that haven't got the integrity or the strength to move your arms and legs effectively.

Running is high impact, your core muscles aren't strong enough to move your arms and legs correctly. Also if you do stomach crunches, these can worsen any abdominal separation. They're not particularly effective at toning up the abdominals, even if you've not had a baby. Walking, using your core muscles in the right posture, is the best way to start; very low impact.

SB: *How do we get our tummy back in shape, assuming you haven't got the abdominal separation?*

VW: Start slowly. Do standing-up work as well as floor core work. You want to target the abdominal muscles. I always recommend the pelvic tilt which brings the abdominals back together again, and going into a bridge, which helps strengthen the glutes.

Squats effectively work your core and your pelvic floor as long as you do them correctly.

At first, you want to focus on exercises which work the transverse abdominus. This is the muscle that wraps around the entire torso. It's a very deep muscle like a corset. Imagine the corset has laces like an old Victorian corset and you're drawing those laces together to tighten that transverse abdominus. You want to be working the muscles from the inside out first, not lots of stomach crunches.

SB: *For running, I do squats and lunges but I don't do anything specifically focusing on abs.*

VW: If you want to get strong for running, it's very important that you do lower-body strength work and work on your glutes. Standing abdominal work is great for runners because you're upright when you run. Teaching your abs to support your spine and doing exercises that involve abdominal work when you're standing is perfect for runners. If you work on your core muscles you can really optimise your performance, and have less risk of injury.

The plank is good as long as you don't have abdominal separation, and your connective tissue is back together. I see many people doing it with poor technique and therefore it's not effective. It's important that technique is good. It's worth seeking out an instructor to see how to do the exercise correctly.

If you are really struggling with time, try and get some childcare or swap with somebody so that you can have some time out; maybe two half-hour slots in your week. Take little steps to build fitness and exercise into your weekly schedule.

Getting the childcare sorted is a really useful way of releasing the stress and not feeling guilty. It's important you have some 'me' time and use it effectively to feel good.

The other thing is the nutrition. Focusing on food and not building exercise into your life is one of the biggest mistakes. Eating well has huge health benefits, but going on a diet isn't going to tone up your muscles and create lean muscle tissue. The more lean muscle tissue you have, the better your metabolism and the more you're going to burn calories at rest.

You can build lean muscle tissue with strength exercises so this isn't cardio. Cardio is great for burning calories, improving your fitness and your energy. As soon as you start strength training, you're burning calories straight away, whereas when you're doing cardiovascular exercise it takes a good 15 minutes to start to burn calories.

Mixing it up makes great sense. You can benefit from great cardiovascular conditioning by doing high intensity but low impact strength exercises.

Squatting for 50 seconds at a fast pace then having a 10-second rest, for example. You get a great work-out, you increase your heart rate, it helps tone you up and improves your metabolism.

My last tip is to take little steps at a time. If you're starting out and you've not done any fitness, or you're scared of fitness instructors, or it seems overwhelming, just get out and start moving more by power walking on different surfaces. Make use of rough terrain or a park, because you will be using your core muscles more effectively on an unstable surface. Get outside, it will make you feel better and lift your spirits, even if it's raining, and start to move more in your day. Build in 15-minute walks every day for the next seven days.

Getting sweaty is off-putting for many mums. You don't have to get sweaty to get a great workout. A good workout will help you achieve leaner, longer muscles and improve your posture as well. It's not about being thin, it's about being fit. Fit and strong and having energy to keep up with your little ones.

Key learning points

1. When you first start to exercise after childbirth, ensure you select a postnatal expert.

2. Prioritise the time – organise childcare swaps or work out with a friend.

3. Build exercise into your weekly schedule.

4. Combine strength training with cardiovascular work to burn more calories.

5. Take small steps at a time, simply getting outside and walking every day is a good start.

Getting fit and being healthy are two great ways to boost your body confidence. For many women, what they wear also has a big impact on their body confidence. Find out more with The Guru Stylist.

Get dressed with confidence

Becky Redpath

People form an impression of us within 30 seconds of meeting. Before we've even said anything. We get one chance to make a great first impression.

Becky Redpath is The Guru Stylist and runs Look Great Feel Fabulous but originally started in nursing. She continues to use the nurturing side of herself to help women feel more confident about the way they look. She has had a passion for fashion, colour and accessories since she was a young girl and bought copies of Vogue with her pocket money. Becky developed the 7 Steps to S.T.Y.L.I.N.G. to help women feel confident and successful in the way they dress.

Although I am not a fashion follower (most comfortable in jeans and a t-shirt), many women do feel very differently about their bodies after childbirth, which impacts on their confidence.

BR: We go through big hormonal changes in our lives and childbirth is one of the biggest. When women go through the menopause, their body changes again. It's about adapting and sometimes that's where women struggle.

To simplify things I developed the '7 Steps to S.T.Y.L.I.N.G. for confidence and success' formula.

First step – the ***significance of positive first impressions***. People form an impression of us within 30 seconds of meeting. Before we've even said anything. We get one chance to make a great first impression so it's an important thing to consider.

The second step is ***target your personal colour palette***. Colour is the easiest and cheapest facelift there is. When you wear the right colours, it can make a real difference to the way you look. Your skin looks more vibrant and you tend to look more youthful. Wearing the wrong colours for our skin tone tends to make us look drawn and tired.

Think about the colours you associate with a sunny autumn day: rich reds, oranges, yellows. Those are warm colours. Cool colours have a blue undertone, the colours you associate with a winter's day: snow, icy shades of blue and grey, pink.

Establish your skin tone and what colours complement you. Women often are a little bit reticent about colour but having your colours doesn't have to mean a whole change of wardrobe. A very simple change such as a scarf around the neck can make a big difference to the way you look.

Colour analysis has been around a long time. An artist in the early 1900s first recognised that his students instinctively painted in the colour palette that complemented their skin tone. He went on to develop colour analysis based on this. There is something about us being drawn to the colours that suit us best.

Third step is *your **style personality***. The clothes we are drawn to are determined by our style personality. Everyone has a style personality: city chic, creative, romantic, dramatic, classic, lateral, fashionista, or the rock chick. When you walk into a shop you will be naturally drawn to certain clothes.

My style personality is city chic so I love tailored clothes, I like to wear heels. Think about what you would wear if your budget was limitless. That's how you determine style personality.

Fourth step is ***love your body shape profile***. I developed body shape profiling and work with 14 body shapes which take into account the nuances in women's shapes.

You can be the same dress size as your best friend but she'll look great in skinny jeans and you don't, or vice versa. Our body shapes are different.

My body shape profiles are named after fruit and vegetables, for example the classic apple. Typically apples have a tummy that's larger than their bust. Quite often their bust tends to sit just on top on their tummies; they have average size busts; quite flat bottoms, not particularly rounded. They have reasonably good legs.

Often they make the mistake of trying to cover up their tummies so they'll wear big baggy shirts. As their legs tend to be slim, they'll wear tapered, narrow trousers so the overall effect emphasises the tummy. They would be much better to choose something like a duster coat, and a top with contrast in colour underneath and matching trousers. This breaks up the expanse of tummy and the apple looks slimmer.

Another example is the leek – they tend to be tall and skinny particularly when they're younger, typically with a lack of definition at the waist. Leeks can be angular at the shoulders with small busts. They need to avoid things that emphasise that shape and introduce fluidity and movement into their clothes so it gives the impression of curves beneath.

Next – *inexpensively add wow! factor to all your outfits*: it's all about accessories. It's an inexpensive, easy way to add interest and personality to your outfits, for example a patterned scarf with at least three colours. Pick a scarf that includes the colour of what you are wearing on your top half and your bottom half, plus at least one or two other colours.

It pulls your whole outfit together and makes a big difference compared to a plain scarf.

Or add a long pendant necklace. Kate Moss is brilliant at accessorising. Her style personality is rock chick, she loves denim and t-shirts. She uses accessories really well: scarfs, belts, pendants, bags, and sunglasses.

The sixth step is **nailing the wardrobe basics** – these are your building blocks. A skirt, a pair of trousers, a pair of dark jeans, a dress, and a couple of tops. Then you bring in colour with tops, knitwear, and accessories such as scarves to pull the outfits together.

The final step is **gorgeous hair and makeup**. Some women shy away from makeup but if you're working or going out, it adds the finishing touch. It doesn't have to be complicated. Your makeup is only as good as your skin care routine, which can be very quick. I use a cleanser and an exfoliator in one. I massage it into my face before I jump into the shower, shower it off and moisturise. And be sure to wear SPF30 to protect your skin, even in the winter.

Key learning points

1. Positive first impressions count.

2. Discover your personal colour palette – the wrong colours can drain you.

3. Identify your natural style personality.

4. Learn to love and dress your body shape profile.

5. Add the wow factor with accessories.

6. Ensure you have your wardrobe basics as you building blocks.

7. Finish it off with gorgeous hair and makeup.

Section Three

Additional Resources

This section includes a number of additional resources and exercises, which are available online for download at www.theconfidentmother.co.uk/book/extras.

I share a bibliography of books that have influenced my journey, as well as books that influenced the many inspirational speakers.

Downloadable content from www.theconfidentmother. co.uk/book/extras:

Additional downloadable content is available at **www.theconfidentmother.co.uk/book/extras**,   much of which is completely free of charge:

- **Core Values** worksheet – a quick and easy method to identify your personal core values.

- **Flexible Working Rights** worksheet provides information on the current UK law with regards to flexible working; types of flexible working; and how to make a successful request.

- **Shared Parental Leave** worksheet provides information on the changes in UK law (December 2014) which affect shared parental leave and came into effect in April 2015.

- **Confident Mother** workbook – a five-page work-book to help you identify what small steps you can take today to be a more confident mother.

- **Confident Mother meal planner** – if you struggle for inspiration in the kitchen, try my one-month meal plan.

You can also purchase **The Confident Mother** library online, which includes the full set of complete interviews from The Confident Mother 2015 conference as well as all the interviews conducted throughout the rest of the year. Use **Book15** for a bonus 15% discount.

Five secrets to being a confident mother

The five secrets we learned over the course of The Confident Mother:

1. **Self-love**

   You need to love yourself, i.e. show yourself compassion in your thoughts and feelings. It is ok to take 'me' time; in fact it is *essential* to nurture yourself. Do you recognise your stress triggers? Have a list of coping strategies available – for some that might be a deep bath with candles, for others a brisk walk round the block, five minutes dancing to loud music or simply a good cup of tea in peace and quiet. Remember that children learn from what we do rather than what we say. Try meditation and practise mindfulness.

2. **Be fully present**

   When we say be fully present when you are with your children, that means giving them your full attention. We all know what it feels like when somebody is only half listening. Don't waste time on feeling guilty or worrying about how little time you have, simply enjoy the time you do have. Being present means not checking your email when you are reading the bedtime story; preparing and eating meals together; giving your child time to talk. It doesn't mean that you have to give all your attention all the time. However it is especially important in the early years to be fully present during times of bodily care, e.g. doing nappy changes or feeding your child.

3. **Forgiveness**

When things go wrong, forgive yourself and forgive others. You don't need to be the perfect mother; good enough really is good enough. If you get it wrong, say sorry. And if you are tired and grumpy, then say so. You don't need to hide your feelings to 'protect' your child. It makes sense to acknowledge your feelings and to model this to your child.

4. **Focus on what is most important**

Do you do too much because you are trying to please everybody? Take time to think about what is most important **to you** and focus on that first.

5. **Hug somebody for 20 seconds every day**

A hug that lasts 20 seconds releases oxytocin (aka the 'happy hormone') which helps you to feel calm and relaxed. This reduces the stress levels in you AND in your child. A simple hug every day increases happiness.

Good enough really is good enough.

How to be a Confident Mother

Here are the questions to ask yourself to take you forward on your journey to be The Confident Mother. I encourage you to find yourself a quiet time of day to complete these questions.

Allow yourself 20–30 minutes. Before you start, close your eyes, and notice how you are feeling. Do three deep breaths in and out. Then open your eyes and start.

What does it mean to you to be a Confident Mother?

What are the benefits of being a Confident Mother?

What to you is THE most important thing about being a Confident Mother?

What do you do now that is important to you as a Confident Mother?

What else would you like to do to be a Confident Mother?

What, if anything, is holding you back from being a Confident Mother?

What are your beliefs about being a Confident Mother?

What beliefs do you hold that are not based on evidence or facts?

What do you want to change?

What support or resources do you need to make that change?

What actions will you take forward?

How to work with Sherry Bevan, The Confidence Guide

I use my inner strength and confidence to nurture and inspire mums like you to make life-changing decisions with ease. You have read my story. You know that I am an action-taker. I don't stop with the decisions. I know exactly how to help you overcome the confidence blocks and inertia that are keeping you stuck. I want women to feel powerful. I will show you how to develop confidence, knowledge and self-understanding so that you feel powerful and take back control of your life.

Your life-changing decision might be charged with emotion; maybe you're scared; perhaps it feels too big to face alone, yet family and friends can't be objective. I provide a safe space to explore your options without judging you. I remove the barriers without scaring you.

Here's how you can work with me...

One-to-one coaching:
You know you are at a crossroads but you are not sure which path to take. You want to make those difficult decisions

with ease, with confidence and with clarity. You want to feel less stressed so that you have more energy. My straight-forward and practical one-to-one coaching over a 3 month (or longer) period will overcome the confidence blocks and inertia that are keeping you stuck.

VIP Day:

If you're really serious about increasing your business con-fidence AND fast; if you lack clarity and focus, you're feel-ing overwhelmed and struggling, you want to increase your business confidence, make the right business decisions so that you have more energy, reduce your stress levels, feel less overwhelm, create a business-family-life balance, AND you know you need one-on-one attention in a concentrated way to keep you focused, the VIP Day is for you.

Business Mastermind:

Are you already running your own business and want to take it to the next level? My Business Confident success and growth programme (also known as a mastermind or busi-ness empowerment programme) is specifically for mums running their own business. This small intimate group is open to no more than six businesses in any 12-month pro-gramme. You can start in February, June or October.

The Confidence Oasis is the monthly membership ver-sion of my Mastermind. You get fantastic content at great value with exclusive access to members-only content, although without the same level of dedicated and interac-tive support from me.

Social Media:

Join me on Facebook: www.facebook.com/Sherry-BevanConsulting and in www.facebook.com/groups/confidentbusinessmums/

On Twitter: @SherryRB

Check out my profile on LinkedIn: https://uk.linkedin.com/in/sherrybevan

Pinterest: www.pinterest.com/sherrybevan1/

YouTube: www.youtube.com/user/SherryBevan

Speakers

Here is a complete list of speakers and their websites, where appropriate.

- Carole Arnold, Adoption Champion
- Toni Brodelle, www.facebook.com/theworldofincredibleme
- Sarah Buchanan-Smith, The Kitchen Table Consultant, www.thekitchentableconsultant.com
- Lucinda Button, Founder of Mamaspace at www.mindfulmamas.co.uk
- Richard Curtis, The Kid Calmer, www.thekidcalmer.com
- Lucy Grainge, Nutritional Therapist, The Food Owl, www.foodowl.co.uk
- Elaine Halligan and Melissa Hood, Positive Parenting Experts, www.theparentpractice.com
- Maxine Harley, Mind Healer, http://maxineharley.com
- Julia Harris, Success Coach and Business Mentor, www.julia-harris.com
- Susan Heaton Wright, Voice Coach, www.executivevoice.co.uk and www.vivalivemusic.com

- Miriam McCaleb, Baby Geek, http://baby.geek.nz

- Dorothy Marlen, Early Childhood Consultant and Trainer, www.dorothymarlen.net

- Naomi Martell-Bundock, The Mindset Mentor, www.coresense.co.uk

- Emily Miller, LinkedIn Tutors, Marshall Walker, www.linkedintutors.com/

- Nicola Mullarkey, The Honest Recruiter, http://thehonestrecruiter.com

- Becky Redpath, Style Guru, www.lookgreatfeelfabulous.co.uk/author/ becky-redpath

- Emma Sargent, Entrepreneur, www.theextraordinarycoachingcompany.com

- Vivienne Smith, Coach and author of *The Single Mum's Survival Guide*, www. thesinglemumssurvivalguide.com

- Dame Sarah Storey, Paralympic Cyclist, www.teamstoreysport.com

- Jo Swinson, former MP and former Minister for Employment Relations and Consumer Affairs, www.joswinson.org.uk/

- Vicky Warr, Postnatal Fitness Expert, www.beezkneezhive.com

- Philippa Williams, Recruitment Consultant, www.capabilityjane.com

Useful Online Resources

Adoption UK – the leading UK charity providing support, awareness and understanding for those parenting or supporting children who cannot live with their birth parents: www.adoptionuk.org/.

Attachment Parenting International: www.attachment-parenting.org.

BLISS – charity supporting parents of babies born too soon, too small or too sick: www.bliss.org.uk/.

Brainwave Trust – a not-for-profit organisation whose aim is to spread awareness and educate the New Zealand community about the latest scientific research on early brain development: www.brainwave.org.nz/.

Down's Syndrome Association – supporting people with Down's syndrome throughout their lives: www.downs-syndrome.org.uk/.

Gingerbread – charity providing expert advice and practical support for single parents: www.gingerbread.org.uk/.

International Emmi Pikler Foundation: http://pikler.org.

National Deaf Children's Society – the leading charity dedicated to creating a world without barriers for deaf children and young people: www.ndcs.org.uk/.

NCT – the UK's leading parenting charity: www.nct.org.uk.

PACT (Parents And Children Together) – one of the UK's leading Voluntary Adoption Agencies: www.pactcharity. org/about-adoption.

Single Parent.org.uk – run by Single Parent Action Network: www.singleparents.org.uk.

Steiner Waldorf Schools Fellowship: www.steinerwaldorf.org/.

Tommy's – funding research into stillbirth, premature birth and miscarriage, and providing information for parents-to-be: www.tommys.org/.

Bibliography

Aiken, Cara (2000) *Surviving Post-natal Depression: At Home No One Hears You Scream.* London: Jessica Kingsley Publishers.

Axline, Virginia M. (1964) *Dibs: in search of self.* New York, USA: Ballantine Books.

Blaffer Hardy, Sarah (1999) *Mother Nature: a history of mothers, infants, and natural selection.* New York, USA: Pantheon Books.

Brown, Laurene Krasny (1986) *Dinosaurs Divorce: A Guide for Changing Families.* Boston, USA: Little, Brown and Company.

Carson, R. (2003) *Taming Your Gremlin: a surprisingly simple method for getting out of your own way.* Rev. edn. New York, USA: Harper Collins.

Cusk, Rachel (2008) *A Life's Work.* London: Faber & Faber.

Enright, Anne (2005) *Making Babies: Stumbling into Motherhood.* London: Jonathan Cape.

De Board, Robert. (1997) *Counselling for Toads: a psychological adventure.* London: Routledge.

Dweck, Carol S. (2006) *Mindset. How You Can Fulfil Your Potential.* New York, USA: Ballantine Books.

Gerhardt, Sue (2004) *Why Love Matters: How Affection*

Shapes a Baby's Brain. Abingdon: Taylor & Francis Ltd.

Goddard Blythe, Sally (2005) *The Well Balanced Child: Movement and Early Learning (Early Years)*. Stroud: Hawthorn Press.

Hartley, Mary (2006) *How To Listen: so that people talk.* London: Sheldon Press.

Hendricks, Gay (2009) *The Big Leap: Conquer Your Hidden Fear and Take Life to the Next Level*. New York, USA: HarperCollins Publishers.

Jackson, Deborah (1989) *Three In A Bed: why you should sleep with your baby.* London: Bloomsbury Publishing.

Liedloff, Jean (1974) *The Continuum Concept: in search of happiness lost*. Rev. edn. 1986. London: Penguin Books.

Lorde, Audre (2007) *Sister Outsider: Essays and Speeches (Crossing Press Feminist Series)*. New York, USA: Ten Speed Press.

Moore-Mallinos, Jennifer (2008) *My Friend Has Down's Syndrome (Let's Talk About It!)* Barron's Educational Series Inc, USA.

Payne, Kim John (2010) *Using the Extraordinary Power of Less to Raise Calmer, Happier, and More Secure Kids*. New York, USA: Ballantine Books.

Perry, Bruce D. with Szalavitz, Maia (2006) *The Boy Who Was Raised As A Dog: What Traumatized Children Can Teach Us About Loss, Love and Healing*. Philadelphia, USA: Basic Books.

Perry, Bruce D. (2006) 'The Neurosequential Model of Therapeutics: Applying principles of neuroscience to clinical work with traumatized and maltreated children' in *Working with Traumatized Youth in Child Welfare*. Ed. Nancy Boyd Webb, The Guilford Press, New York, NY, pp. 27-52.

Shore, Rima (2003) *Rethinking The Brain*. Families and Work Institute.

Siegel, Daniel J. (2015) *The Developing Mind: How Relationships and the Brain Interact to Shape Who We Are*. New York, USA: The Guilford Press.

Stadlen, Naomi (2011) *How Mothers Love: and how relationships are born*. London: Piatkus.

Sunderland, Margot (2007) *What Every Parent Needs to Know: The incredible effects of love, nurture and play on your child's development*. London: Dorling Kindersley.

Syed, Matthew (2010) *Bounce: The Myth of Talent and the Power of Practice*. New York, USA: HarperCollins Publishers.

Tolle, Eckhart (1999) *The Power of Now: A Guide to Spiritual Enlightenment*. Novato, CA, USA: New World Library.

Tsabary, Dr Shefali (2015) *The Conscious Parent: Transforming ourselves, empowering our children*. London: Yellow Kite.

Lightning Source UK Ltd.
Milton Keynes UK
UKOW06f1056070915

258200UK00002B/44/P